Jack McArdle ss cc

150 Stories
for Preachers and Teachers

THE COLUMBA PRESS
DUBLIN

First Edition, 1990, published by
THE COLUMBA PRESS
93 The Rise, Mount Merrion, Blackrock, Co Dublin, Ireland

Designed by Bill Bolger
Origination by The Columba Press
Printed in Ireland by
Mount Salus Press Ltd, Dublin.

ISBN: 0 948183 91 8]

A number of these stories come from 'Christianity is ... People who need help' by James F Colaianni and published in 1977 by Liturgy Publications Inc, Silver Spring, MD.

Contents

Thematic Index

The references here are to the story numbers.

Introduction

Jesus was a great storyteller and I have always believed that there is a child hidden in the heart of each of us, so that we all love a story. Especially a story that teaches, that lingers, that lasts, that causes us to think a little bit deeper.

I'm not sure exactly if I have any particular purpose in putting together some of these stories, beyond hoping to help people to reflect. I don't want them to be some kind of a stopgap for a preacher because, if it's not coming from the speaker's heart, it's not going to touch the listener's heart. However I pray that in some little way the stories that follow will enable some people just to think a little deeper, look again at the same truth from a different angle, because the gospel doesn't change. Perhaps we'll be willing to learn more of what I believe God wants us to know.

The stories are arranged under ten general subject headings, although, of course, some of them could be included in a number of sections, and even in sections which don't appear here at all.

In order to be as helpful as possible to the user, I have also drawn up a Thematic Index for reference purposes. Again, many of the stories could be included in other sections, but I hope you will find this index helpful, for all its weaknesses.

Finally, a word of thanks to all those people everywhere who have the time and the talent to come up with original stories which all of us can then use in our task of spreading the Good News. Particular thanks to the composers and adapters of the stories included in this book. I really can't remember where half of them came from, and I hope that this general thanks and acknowledgement will suffice.

Jack McArdle ss cc
Word Peace Day 1990

Jesus, the Way, the Truth, the Life

1 There was this dark cave down in the ground, down under the earth. Obviously it had never seen light, and therefore wouldn't know what light was. And one day, the sun invited it to come up and visit. When the cave came up to visit the sun it was amazed and delighted, because the cave had never seen light before. Naturally, the cave felt obligated and invited the sun to come down to visit it sometime, because the sun had never seen darkness. So the day came and the sun came down and was ushered into the cave and, as the sun came into the cave, it looked around and, rather puzzled, said, 'Where is the darkness?' because there wasn't any there.

Once you open your heart to God and invite his light to come into your darkness, the Lord himself, who called himself the Light of the World, will look around and say, 'Where's the darkness?'

2 *The idea of going to heaven is something that must be spoken about again and again. It's a totally free gift. I am going to heaven because Jesus died to get me there. My vocation, my particular vocation as a priest, for example, is not to go round to save anyone but to go round to tell people they're saved. My vocation is not to work towards getting people into heaven but to do whatever I can to get heaven into people. And it is more difficult, I can assure you, to get heaven into people than to get people into heaven. But you cannot earn it – a totally free gift. There is no place for muscular Christianity or members of the 'white knuckle club' if you want to get to heaven.*

There was a teacher who died recently and went to heaven.

He went to the door and Peter said, 'Hold there! Come here! Where are you going?' 'I'm going in there' 'Oh, no you're not.' 'Why not?' 'It's not that simple.' 'Why?' 'Well, we have a points system here you see, so many points to get in.' And the teacher said: 'Oh, I didn't think that applied here.' 'Well, we're trying it out.' said Peter. 'How many points,' said the teacher, 'to get in?' 'Well, you need a thousand, actually,' said Peter. So the teacher was taken aback a little bit, but then he rallied and Peter said, 'O.K.! Come on, come on, what did you do when you were down there?' So he stuck out his chest and he said, 'I went to Mass every morning for forty years.' This was his 'biggie', you know! And Peter said, 'Fair enough. That's one point.' At this stage your man's heart was in his boots and Peter said, 'What else?' 'Well I belonged to the Third World agencies, Vincent de Paul Society and all.' And Peter said, 'Come on, stop waffling! There's people behind you! How much did you get?' 'Probably, over the years I was in fund-raising, twenty, twenty-five thousand.' 'Very good, very good, ' said Peter, 'Not bad. That's another point' At this of course, your man was totally deflated and he muttered to himself, something like, 'It's only by the grace of God I'm going to get in there.' And Peter turned to him and said, 'Once you believe that, that's the thousand points. Now if you believe that, then you can go on in. Because it is a total, absolute, pure free gift.'

---

3   One night a man dreamed he was walking along the beach with the Lord. Across the sky flashed scenes from his life. For each scene, he noticed two sets of footprints in the sand, one belonging to him and the other to the Lord.

When the last scene of his life flashed before him, he looked back at the footprints in the sand. He noticed that many times along the path of his life, there was only one set of footprints. He also noticed that it happened at the very lowest and saddest times of his life.

This really bothered him and he questioned the Lord about it: 'Lord, you said that once I decided to follow you, you'd walk with me all the way. But I have noticed that during the most troublesome times in my life, there is only one set of footprints. I don't understand why, when I needed you most, you would leave me.'

The Lord replied, 'My precious, precious child, I love you and I would never leave you during your times of trial and suffering. When you see only one set of footprints, it was then that I carried you.'

4   *To realise that God himself came down among us, to ex- perience and to share our weakness, is to understand something that is at the very heart of Incarnation. On a human level it didn't make any sense, because the world doesn't understand the power that there is in littleness. And when Jesus came as a helpless infant, the Herods of this world were really scared because they can't deal with that. The world would have to shoot a Mahatma Ghandi or a Martin Luther King because there is a power in that kind of strength that the bully dimension of the world can't deal with in any other way.*

One Christmas Eve, a man was wondering why God chose to come down as a helpless infant. As he was thinking about this, he heard some noise outside his window and he looked out. He saw that some green geese had landed in his back garden. The snow had drifted and they had landed in the snow. Flying in from the North Pole to the Gulf of Mexico, one of them had got injured and, as is the habit with green geese when they fly in formation, if one of them is injured some others will come down and not abandon him. So this man, more heart than head, ran out to help. Once he appeared, of course, he scared the life out of them and they began to flounder and sink into the snow, injuring themselves. He opened the garage door, trying to shoost them to go into the garage, hoping that he might get some Society for the Protection of Green Geese, (I am sure you could find such a group somewhere!) that

9

might come along and help. But the more he tried to get the geese into the garage, the more harm he was doing and the more they were injured. For one crazy moment he wished he was a goose, and then he could speak their language and tell them that he was only trying to help! And then it dawned on him why Jesus came the way he did!

He came as a helpless infant to be like one of us, so that he could speak our language. He could actually touch the child and forgive the sinner and feed the hungry and show us exactly what we ourselves had to do.

5

One time a group of men were sitting around and talking about good and bad memories. As a result of the discussion, a wager was put on about reciting something, and one young lad stood up and recited, 'The Lord is my shepherd, there is nothing I shall want.' He had some dramatic training and delivery and diction, and was very, very effective and he had to recite the psalm a second and a third time to thunderous applause. The second man was elderly and stooped and it was difficult to hear him. He was bent down and, away over in the corner, he recited, 'The Lord is my shepherd, there is nothing I shall want.' And when he was finished there was total silence around the room, as each man bowed his head and began to pray quietly to himself. The young lad who recited the psalm the first time, explained the two totally different receptions to the same psalm, and he said, 'It's fairly obvious that I know the psalm, but that old man knows the shepherd.'

The problem with us is that we know the psalm. We have learned all the answers, but we mightn't know the shepherd. If I don't know the shepherd, (because Christianity is about a person, Jesus Christ), then nobody will pray when I speak.

6 *To be a Christian is to develop a family resemblance, so that the Spirit that was in Christ continues to work in us. In other words, to be Christ to others and to see Christ in others.*

There was a group of guys once coming back from a computer conference. They were dashing back by taxi to a railway station to get the train to the next town. The train was about to pull away as they jumped out of the taxi. They ran across the platform to jump on the train and one of the guys accidentally hit a table with some apples on it. There was someone there selling the apples.

Now one guy was in the process of becoming a Christian. We never actually become Christians. We are always, as Chesterton says, 'in the process of becoming', so this man was trying to become a Christian. It wasn't he who hit the table but that didn't matter. He jumped off the train and said to the others, 'I'll catch up with you along the way. Off you go.' When he came back he was surpised to find that there was a young lad sitting at the table with some apples scattered on the ground. The young lad was about eight years of age and he was blind. He was waiting for his mother to come back, for she had gone across the road to buy something in the shop. The man picked up the apples, stacked them up neatly, put some that were damaged to one side. He put his hand in his pocket and gave the young lad some money and said, 'I'm sorry for what has happened. I hope we haven't spoiled your day. And God bless you.' And as he turned to walk away, the young lad who was blind and who couldn't see him, turned in his direction and said, 'Sir!' 'Yes?' 'Are you Jesus?'

Jesus says, 'Who do you say that I am?' Because how you act towards others, whether you are moody, impatient, intolerant, arrogant, you are my ambassadors, you are my representatives. Who do you say that I am? You see, what matters is not what we do, it is why we do it.

7 On one of the San Francisco streets there is a funeral parlour with some beige curtains covering the windows. In front of the curtains there is a sign which reads, 'Why walk around half dead when we can bury you for ninety eight bucks?'

There's a better way to ask the question, and everyone of the biblical writers, each in his own way, asked the very same question, 'Why do you walk around half dead when there is a way of replenishing your strength?' You see there is a great difference between living and existing. Everybody dies but not everybody lives. Some people just exist and, when they die, you have to get in a doctor to certify they are dead because you can't notice any difference – there was never much life there anyhow!

8 A few years ago, a news photographer won an award for a picture of death which he had taken. A young woman was found dead in a sportscar. She had died from an overdose of narcotics. Using a wide-angle lens, the cameraman produced a photograph showing not only the body, pitifully sprawled across the front seat of the car, but also the parking meter which read 'time expired'.

It was a haunting and grim reminder of the inevitability of death. We will all die; everyone we love will die; each day in some new way we are being reminded that we are just a heart-beat away from death. Inevitably the epitaph, 'time expired', applies to us all.

9 A very holy man had served for many years in a big downtown parish, and he decided to shift gears in his middle age by settling down as a pastor to a small rural congregation. It occured many years ago, but this is the way he still tells the story of his first big country meal in a parishioner's home:

'The eating was good; it was almost sinful: baked ham and

fried chicken and roast beef, sweet potatoes and mashed potatoes, vegetable casseroles fairly dripping with butter, fresh-baked bread and rolls and, for desert, hot blueberry pie topped with huge wedges of homemade vanilla icecream. All through that meal something was bothering me. I just couldn't enjoy it. All during the dinner, I heard the obvious sound of running water and it really bugged me. Back in the city, that sound was bad news. Someone had left a tap running and the sink or tub was about to overflow, or there was a leak in the plumbing and the ceiling was about to cave in. For two hours I listened to little else but that sound of running water. However, since it was my first visit to the parishioner's home, I was reluctant to say anything. Finally I could no longer contain myself, so I asked about it. With a smile, my host explained the situation to me. It seems that forty years before, when the people had built the farmhouse, they discovered a spring of water right in the centre of their property. So they built a spring room around it and then designed the house around the spring room. For forty years, the people who lived in the house had been refreshed and nourished by this spring of water that was welling up right at the centre of their home. I thought to myself, "This is what Jesus is constantly trying to tell us: that it is possible for us to build the rooms of our lives around the life-giving spring wa ter of God's grace."

10

Following Jesus is walking in his way, not changing the signs or altering the rules. He didn't say he was one of the ways; he said, 'I am the Way.'
There was a man one time who set out on a walking trip to the town of Shadeyville. Arriving at a fork in the road, he was annoyed to discover a signpost with two arrows. One pointed to a wide and smoothly paved road and the other, marked 'Shadeyville', pointed to a narrow, mucky, unpaved trail. Suddenly he had a bright idea. He climbed up the post, reversed the signs and proceeded merrily on his way along the smooth road. Of course he never reached Shadeyville.

11 *The role of the Church is to lead people to God. The role of John the Baptist was to point to Jesus, to be a signpost.*
A certain Rabbi once shocked his congregation by saying that Moses was not really much of a leader. They really woke up when he made this statement, which is unthinkable to any Jewish audience. The Rabbi went on to explain that if, when Moses led the people out of Egypt, he had turned right instead of left, we would have the oil and they would have the desert.

But Moses was a good leader; he knew what he was doing. In fact, that's the beauty of the Old Testament story about the Exodus: Moses led the people into the desert and that is where they found God.

12 *The power to trust will guide you over the pits of aimlessness and despair. Despair is the ultimate, real sin for the Christian.*
There is a famous old story about a Rabbi who was coming to the Day of Atonement in a state of deep depression. The Day of Atonement, in the tradition of the Hebrew people, is a day of repentance and restoration. He was depressed, lethargic, and fatigued. He was feeling very, very low. He was standing in the doorway of his little house, and down the road came a cobbler, pushing his cart with his tools and his materials on it. When the cobbler came opposite the Rabbi's house and saw him standing in the doorway, he shouted in a very loud voice, 'Do you have anything that needs mending?' The Rabbi said it was like the voice of God, because he suddenly saw so clearly what the source of his problem really was. 'Do you have anything that needs mending?'

13

I remember hearing, years ago, about a guy in my own part of the country. He was a simple soul, was in the front seat of every church, chapel, and meeting. And one day, there was a preacher up on the back of a truck, down in the town square, thumping a Bible and talking about finding the Lord. As usual, Sam was in the front row looking up, and he had that vacant look that, to the stranger, might seem like some sort of ecstacy or deep religious emotion. So the preacher turned to him and he said, 'My dear man, have you found the Lord?' And Sam says, 'No, did you lose him?'

For once Sam was brilliant! It was the question that was stupid. We don't lose God. We are the ones who are always getting lost.

14

Jesus came that we should have life and have it more abundantly. I think it was St Irenaeus who said one time that the glory of God is man fully alive.

Someone asked Flannery O'Connor, on one of her campus lecture tours, 'Do you feel that Universities stifle writers?' She replied, 'I feel they don't stifle enough writers'.

There is a similar story in which the question is asked, 'Do the theological seminaries stifle preachers?' And the answer is 'Seminaries don't stifle enough preachers!'

There are too many lifeless writers, there are too many lifeless preachers, there are too many lifeless business people, there are too many lifeless teachers, there are too many lifeless parents. God loves us so much that when he calls us into life in his great goodness he gives us two births. A birth that brings us into this world and then a birth that brings us into life. 'I came that you should have life and have it more abundantly.'

15

Peace, we often heard it said, is not the absence of war. It's the presence of something. Nor is love the absence of hatred.

A man came home from a very tough day at the office, and he said to his wife, 'I've had a bad day. Please, if you've any bad news tonight, keep it to yourself!' To which she replied, 'O.K. No bad news. Now for the good news. Remember our four children? Well, three of them didn't break an arm today!'

16

There can be a difference between 'getting lost' and 'going astray'. Quite often in life we can go astray. But being lost is quite different.

There is a story told of a man on a journey to a distant city. Being unfamiliar with the route, he became confused and took the wrong road. When he realised his predicament, he stopped his car and asked a passing stranger, 'Can you help me? I'm lost.' 'Where are you going to?' the stranger asked. 'Going to Dublin,' to which the stranger replied, 'Then you're not lost. You know where you are going. All you need is directions.'

17

It has to be said again and again that Christianity is about a person, Jesus Christ.

There is an old church in Sweden that's historically important for several reasons, but the thing that strikes the visitor most is the life-like crucifix on the wall at the back of the church. It hangs directly opposite the pulpit where the preacher can see it, but where the people cannot. When the guide is asked why the crucifix is at the back, rather than up front where everybody can see it, he tells this story.

One Sunday, King Charles XII made an unexpected visit to

the church. When the preacher saw the king come in, he threw away his prepared sermon and spent the time talking about the king's virtues and how much he was doing for his people. A few days later, the crucifix arrived at the church as a gift from the king. Along with it came a letter in which the king ordered that the crucifix be placed on the wall opposite the pulpit, so that from then on, anyone who mounted that pulpit to preach would be reminded of the one he was supposed to be talking about.

18

'There is no one good but God', says Jesus to the rich young man. In other words, only God is perfect. You don't love someone who is perfect, you adore him.

In Alan Paton's novel, *Cry the Beloved Country,* there is a young man who is born late in his parents' lives. He leaves his home in the hill country and goes down to the city. He never writes or sends back news. Finally, his elderly father decides to go to the city to find him. Not accustomed to city life, the father becomes bewildered and confused, and he doesn't know which way to turn. Then a minister in the town hears his story and resolves to help him. The old man moves in with the minister, who goes out of his way to try to help the father to pick up clues, get on the trail of the boy. And when they seem to be making progress, the old man, with tears in his eyes, is trying thank the minister for all he has done. He can't quite find the words. He simply says, 'You're a good man.' The minister replies, 'I'm not a good man. I'm a sinful and a selfish man. But Jesus Christ has laid his hands on me, that's all.'

19

Have you ever heard the phrase 'get off my back'? And yet Jesus is more or less saying, 'Come to me. Get on my back, I'll carry you.'

These are lines from a song that was made popular a few years ago by a British rock group called *The Hollies*:

I'm strong, strong enough to carry him
He ain't heavy, he's my brother.

20 Myra had worked for many years in a large, down-town business office. Many different things were said about Myra, but on one point all her colleagues agreed: Myra was a hateful person. No one had ever managed to get close enough to her to know her very well. She had a way of quickly turning off anyone who tried to befriend her. She was a loner, and a disagreeable one at that. Consequently whenever a new employee was hired, the warning went out, 'Stay away from Myra'. This situation lasted for years until a new employee, whom we shall call Margaret, arrived on the scene. Disregarding all the friendly warnings, Margaret made a special effort to let Myra know that now there was someone in that office who really cared about her. Amazingly, this initial expression of kindness eventually began to bear fruit. Myra was breaking out of her shell. She was communicating more easily . She even was developing a friendship or two. Then, early one morning, the entire office staff was shocked to learn that Margaret had died suddenly the night before. When Myra heard the news she cried and cried and said over and over again, 'Margaret was the only Christ I ever knew, she was the only Christ I ever knew.'

It is not at all surprising to hear some one spontaneously associating an act of love and compassion such as this with Jesus and his followers. Christianity, after all, is not only a way of thinking but it is a way of living.

21 There was a young lad who grew up by the seaside. He had a real love of, and fascination with boats. He got a small block of timber and began to carve a model boat for himself. This boat was going to be just perfect, because it would represent everything beautiful that he had ever seen in boats. When he was finished, he painted it his favourite colour, and he even put his own name on it. Then he rigged up tiny sails, and the labour of love was complete.

It would not be a real boat, he thought, unless he put it into the water. So, down to the sea he went and he watched proudly as it bobbed about on the waves. He was proud of it, and was so lost in his admiration that it was some time before he realised what was heppening. He had given it sails and the wind was blowing it firmly but gently further and further away from him. He called out to it, as if it should obey him, but it was now under another influence. He watched in horror and great pain as it drifted away out to sea.

He was really upset when he got home and he didn't sleep too much that night. Then, one day, he was passing a toy shop, and was jolted out of his depression by the sight of a toy boat in the window – and, yes, it was his boat! He rushed in eagerly to claim it, but the shopkeeper coldly dismissed his claims, saying that it belonged to him now, and if the boy wanted it, he would have to buy it.

The boy rushed home and told his dad. He wanted to know how much he should pay for it, and the father replied, 'If you really need to get that boat, you will give everything you have to get it.' So the boy emptied out all his savings boxes and ran down to the shop with every penny he had. He landed the money on the counter without even checking it, and rushed back out the door with his beloved boat. He rubbed it, hugged it, and ran to show it to his dad. 'Ah!' says the dad, 'so the boat is yours now.' 'It surely is mine!' says the boy. 'I made it and then bought it back, and gave all I had to get it. It's mine indeed – only now it's mine twice over!'

You are the boat, and Jesus is the boy.

Response to the Gospel

22 There was a minister one time who was going to retire and he decided to build himself a bungalow. He had some spare time and expertise, and he decided to build the bungalow out of the book. He knew what he was about, but there was one problem that he hadn't foreseen. He couldn't hang a door. No matter how he tried with the hinges it just overlapped, scraped, whatever. It got on his nerves and one day he was losing his ministerial dignity, as it were, and he just walked away and left it and went for a walk.

He walked off down the road and, lo and behold, he hadn't gone very far when he came across a place where there was a house being built. There was a carpenter putting on the front door, so this was his chance, and he stood watching. The carpenter became uneasy; he felt there was someone looking at him, and he said, 'Can I help you?' which can be one way of saying, 'get lost'! So the Minister said, 'Well, I'll tell you, this is my problem,' and he told him the problem he had with the house, and, he said, 'that's why I was watching you.'

The carpenter's eyes sparkled for a moment and he said, 'I'll make a bargain with you.' 'What's that?' 'I've been a member of your congregation for years, and every Sunday I have to go along and listen to you. Now I'll put on every door in your house if you'll do something for me.' Seems strange, yeh, O.K., he agreed. The idea of getting every door put on his house was very tempting but he asked, 'What do you want me to do?'

The carpenter said, 'I'll put on every door in your house for you if you'll let me preach you a sermon. The only thing that I will specify is, all the years when I had to listen to you I couldn't interrupt you, I had to listen. Now, you will not be allowed interrupt me.'

Well, it seemed a rather unusual request, but he agreed to it. So the carpenter said, 'O.K. come on!' He got him in the car and drove off down the road, turned left, right, and eventually stopped and brought him in across the long grass and into this place where the foundation of a house had been built some years previously. And for some reason or other it was still that way, with nettles and briars and old broken bottles, whether somebody changed their mind or died, or whatever, I don't know. The minister looked at it and looked at the carpenter and he couldn't ask any questions. So the carpenter just said to him, 'Think about it.'

Then he got him in the car and eventually they came to a house, and as the minister was getting out of the car, he couldn't believe it. He looked at this house – absolutely beautiful, the finish, the decor, the garden, the manicured lawns, the drapes, the front door, everything absolutely perfect. He was escorted up the driveway; the front door was open; he was ushered in and he looked around – absolute amazement, for there was nothing, no ceilings, no walls, no floors, nothing, total shell. He looked at the carpenter in amazement but he couldn't ask a question and the carpenter said, 'Think about it.'

Now there are always three, as you know, so he got him in the car and off they went again. And eventually they pulled up at this house and got out and the minister noticed this house was not bad, not bad – the grass could do with a trim, the gates could do with a lick of paint, the spouting was a bit loose at one side, the drapes on one of the windows a bit crooked ... As the carpenter brought him up to the door, he opened the door and he said, 'I'm home honey,' and a woman came out and gave him a hug and the kids came running out and said, 'Daddy! Daddy!' and dived into his pockets for sweets. The minister was standing at the door and he saw there was a school blazer lying on the floor, and there was a school bag lying on a stairs – but, ah! it wasn't bad. And as he was looking around the carpenter said, 'Oh, sorry, I forgot,' and he said, 'Think about it.'

And the Minister left and thought about it. And according to the story, the following Sunday he gave the greatest sermon of his life. Because he talked about the three things that people do with the message of Jesus Christ:

Some of them, early in life, build a foundation, (what I might call First Communion spirituality,) and they never do a thing with it after that. I knew of a man, still confessing at eighty years of age that he hadn't done what his parents told him – they were dead for years. I had an uncle who said a prayer every night in his night prayers against having a toothache and he hadn't a tooth of his own for years.

The second kind of person is the one who does a fantastic snow job; fantastic external job, everything externally: always there in the front seat, always there at all novenas and gatherings etc., but inside nothing, nothing, emptiness, no hope, jealousy, anger, resentment, nothing inside of God. Externally fantastic.

And the third one – and I'd like to think that that's you and me: in need of a lick of paint, and a trimming or straightening out from time to time here and there, but, a lot of love there.

---

23 *I believe that the road to heaven is heaven. Just like the road to hell is hell. I believe heaven starts now. For someone who doesn't understand that, they might imagine that the road to heaven is hell, they think it's tough; and some other poor people, worse still, could imagine that the road to hell is heaven, it's great fun.*

There was a man one time who was anxious to know what hell and heaven were like and he was taken off to see them. He was very surprised to find that hell consisted of a large room with a long table down the centre, laden down with food: every kind of food you could imagine and people sitting round the table. But each person was in total misery and frustration because each had two 5ft long chop-sticks and wasn't able to get the food up to his mouth.

Then the man was taken in next door to see heaven. And he

was more amazed to find that heaven also consisted of a large room with a long table down the centre, laden down with delicious food, just like the other room. Each person around the table had two 5ft long chop-sticks, but each was completely fulfilled and happy, as they picked up the food with their chop-sticks and fed the person sitting across from them.

24 There was a priest who came to a new parish. (I often joke that every priest has about six sermons, and after that he should be shifted to the next parish before he starts repeating himself!) It was his first sermon and it was great and they were all talking about it all week. So the next Sunday they were hanging out of the lights, and he got up and, guess what, he gave the very same sermon. And well, O.K., that didn't faze anybody, that's understandable; there were people who weren't here last Sunday so it was good he gave the same one.

But on the third, fourth and fifth Sunday, he gave the very same one. That was a little too much, so two little old ladies in tennis shoes were delegated to go round the back, into the sacristy and they were very diplomatic about it. One of them said, 'Father, that's a very good sermon.' And he said, 'Thank you very much, I'm delighted.' 'It's very good, I must say. We liked it very much.' 'That's good. Thank you, thanks for telling me.' 'We were just wondering though, Father...' 'Yes?' 'We were just wondering if you knew that you were giving the same sermon each...' 'Oh, yes, I know that.' 'Well, we were just wondering – I hope you don't mind us asking you – do you have other sermons?' 'Oh I have surely. I have a whole lot more.' 'We were asked to ask you, you know, I hope you won't be offended, but will you be going on to the other sermons sometime?' 'Oh, I will and looking forward to that.' 'We want to be able to tell our friends, Father, when will you be doing that?' And he said, 'Oh, I'll be going on to the next sermon as soon as I see you doing something about the first one.'

And you know, I often think of Paul, in Antioch. He came across the monument to the unknown god and he gave a powerful sermon about this god and who he was. At the end of it all, they said, 'That's very interesting. We must hear him again sometime.' In other words, we are not going to do anything about it.

Peter Calvey hermit says that one of the ways in which you never get round to doing anything is to talk about it long enough.

Or you could arrive at what I call 'paralysis through analysis'. Or, as someone said one time, 'when all is said and done, there's much more said than done'.

25

An awful lot depends on ourselves. It really does. I think in terms of when I was a kid, the excitement that there was because of the 'rural lectric', that's what it was called. I suppose it would be 'rural electrification'. But the 'lectric' was coming and the place was abuzz. The guys from town were telling us that the poles were coming down the main road and then, after a while, the man from the creamery said they were coming in the side road, and each week we got further word that the great days were coming.

Now, as country lads visiting Dublin, we had seen radios that were plugged in and electric switches and hot water and, Wow! this was going to be heaven. And I remember the excitement of it all and yet one thing puzzled me.

There was an elderly couple who lived near me, and they didn't take it. And I couldn't understand that. I didn't understand that you had to apply and sign for it; I thought that they came to put it in. And this couple didn't take it. And for a long time I was puzzled when I saw the candle in the window or the tilleylamp or the hurricane lamp or the oil lamp, and here were electric wires passing their front door.

Now, that is the way it is with God. You don't have to take it. God doesn't give you anything; he just offers it to you.

26 *The idea of religion is an extraordinary thing. It can be quite divorced from a spirituality. Religion can be quite external. Just like Pharisees: very religious people, but as in the morning of Pentecost in Jerusalem, they met people who were spirit-filled and they thought they were drunk.*

I heard of a man who stood up at a prayer meeting and confessed that he had been a drunkard, a wife beater, been unfaithful, aggressive, a jailbird, a robber. You name it, he'd done it. And then he stuck out his chest and he said with all sincerity, 'But I want to thank God that, throughout those years, I never lost my religion!'

27 *They say there are three groups of people in any society, and that includes any parish. There is one group that causes things to happen; there's another group who watch things happening; and there's the vast majority who haven't a clue what's going on!*

It's like a group of people who set out to climb a mountain and when they get to the bottom of the mountain one third of them are tired. They are sorry they came so they are going to sit here and wait till the others come back. The other two-thirds continue to climb and, half way up, there's a plateau and they stop to have picnic. It's a beautiful day, so half of them decide to just lie in the sun and enjoy themselves. The remaining third came to climb the mountain and that's what they do!

28 There was a group of Christians some years ago, in a country where the Church was persecuted. They were praying, and suddenly the door of the room was broken down by the boot of a soldier who walked in with a machine gun. He looked around them and he said, 'Any of you people who does not believe in Christ, get out while you have a chance'. There was silence for a while and gradually, one by one, people began to make for the exits. There was a small group of people there who made up their minds, they knew where they stood. So they stayed where they were. Their decision was already made, not knowing what was going to happen.

The soldier went over and closed the doors, came back and stood in front of them. Then he smiled and said, 'I believe in Jesus too, and we're much better off without them.'

29 A lot of our sins have to do, not with what we do wrong, but in the good things we don't do. In Albert Camus' novel, *The Fall*, there's a devastating line that expresses the truth of how narrow our lives can become. There is a scene where a respectable lawyer, walking in the streets of Amsterdam, hears a cry in the night. He realises that a woman has fallen or has been pushed into the canal and is crying out for help. Then the thoughts come rushing through his mind. Of course he must help, but ... a respected lawyer getting involved in this way, what would the implications be, what about the natural danger ... after all, who knows what has been going on?' By the time he has thought it through, it is too late. He moves on, making all kinds of excuses to justify his failure to act. Camus writes, 'He did not answer the cry for help because that was the kind of man he was.'

30 I remember meeting a young man leaving a rehabilitation centre for alcoholics, some years ago. He had come there only the day before and he was walking out the very next morning. 'Do you know what they wanted me to do in there?' he confided to me in a shocked whisper, 'They wanted me to change my whole life style!' The poor lad saw all that as being far too difficult, and he was getting out of there as fast as he could.

In fact, this man had chosen the more difficult road by far, and the road that had been suggested to him was much, much easier, and held hopes for so much more love and happiness in life than the one that he chose to follow.

31

They say that procrastination is the thief of time; we're always going to do something about something some other time. God is totally a God of now.

There is a story of a man who bought a used suit of clothes at the Goodwill industry store. In one of the pockets he found a fifteen-year-old ticket for a shoe repair job. The store was still doing business at the old neighbourhood location so, as a bit of a joke, the man decided to try to redeem the shoes. When he presented the ticket, the proprietor looked at it for a moment and then disappeared into the back room. A few moments later he reappeared saying very calmly, 'They'll be ready next Tuesday.'

Everything is going to happen next Tuesday! As they say, all diets start on Monday.

32

You know the struggle people have to try to become Christian – the 'white-knuckle club' as I keep calling them. This story teaches us, in a very simple way, a basic lesson about becoming a Christian.

It's the story of a crow, a crow that was very down, droopy, feathers all awry, anorexic-looking and depressed. His pals were very worried about him, so one day one of his friends went to see him to find out what could possibly be bothering him. Very diplomaticaly, but very concerned, he asked him. And the crow admitted to being depressed, being down, a sense of failure, a sense of a wasted life. Life was ticking by and none of his ambitions was going to be fulfilled. As a matter of fact, he confided that he really had only one ambition in life. When he wasn't volunteering the information, his friend asked him what that was. He looked around rather sheepishly and said,

'You won't laugh?'

'No, no, I won't.'

'Well, I want to to be a singer ... to make a record.'

'A record?'

'Yes.'

'What of?'

'Singing.'

The other crow couldn't keep serious, which really infuriated him and he said,

'No wonder I'm down, with people like you laughing at me! Why couldn't I sing? Did you ever hear a blackbird singing? I'm the same colour and I'm bigger than him and of course I could sing. If you knew the trouble I went to to sing like a blackbird – I went to the health shop, changed my bird seed, I got Vivioptel, Royal Jelly. I got the whole lot. And after all my work I got up in a tree and opened my mouth and began and, 'Caaw! caaw!' No. That wasn't going to work. So then I was determined. I got a tape-recorder, got a C90, got up on the tree in the middle of the blackbirds, filled the C90 with all the blackbirds singing. And then I had my walkman with my headphones night and day – subliminal, you know; listened to it; brainwashing. Eventually I was really going to get this right.'

After all his trouble, up he goes in a tree, opens his mouth ...'Caaw! caaw!' He was really, really down, and then he decided to get sheet music, to go for voice training, because he was determined that he was going to sing like a blackbird! After all his expense and all his time and all his effort, up he goes in a tree once again and opens his mouth ... 'Caaw! caaw!'

So he was absolutely in the depths and one morning he picked up a morning paper. Turning over the pages, there was something that caught his eye. There was an article about someone in South Africa, called Christian Barnard, who did transplants. 'Transplants!' The word was magic. That's what it was, a transplant! That's what he needed! He flew home, got on the phone, phoned Christian Barnard.

'Hello, is that you?'

'Yes, it's me.'

'I hear you do transplants,' and he was all excited.

'Yes, yes.'

'What kind of transplants do you do?'

'Well, we do hearts.'

'Any other kind?'

'Well, we do lungs and livers...'

'Do you ever do a voice box?'

'Well, no ...'

'Could you do a voice box?'

'Well, I suppose we could ... it shouldn't be any more difficult than a heart transplant.'

'If I went out there would you try one?'

He seemed so anxious that Christian Barnard said,

'OK! Come ahead.'

So he went out, and they were in touch with the local hospitals and the local mortuaries waiting for a blackbird to keel over, especially one with a donor card. Eventually there was an old blackbird that tipped over and they claimed the voice box. And the crow, at long last, lay back and shut up and let somebody else take over who knew what he was doing, and he had a transplant. And he was now given the voice box of a blackbird.

In no time at all, because he had what it takes, he was up in a tree and he was singing like a blackbird and for the rest of his life he couldn't sing any other way.

Now that's really what it takes. He was able to sing like a blackbird when he had the voice box of a blackbird. And there's no way I can become a Christian without having a transplant. 'I will take out that heart of stone and give you a heart of flesh and I will put my spirit in you.'

33

Revelations 12 says, 'I wish you were either hot or cold. Because you are neither I will vomit you out of my mouth,' which is one way of saying, 'You make me sick!'
One time there was a group of people at a prayer

meeting. There was a fancy dress parade, or a fancy dress ball somewhere in the area and this guy was travelling along and he was dressed as Satan. But, very appropriately, the heavens opened. It rained, it bucketed down and he was walking, so he ran into the nearest doorway. It happened to be a church hall where there was a prayer meeting, and once Satan appeared there was a scurry and a scramble for the exits in all directions. And one little old lady's coat caught in the seat, and, as Satan approached her, she really panicked and she said, 'Satan! I know, I know I went to Mass every morning for the last fifty years, but all the time really, all the time I was on your side!'
It could be true!

34 *Chesterton would say that you never become Christian. You are always in the process of becoming. But one who is 'almost Christian' is someone who never really says a 'yes'. There is always a holdback.*

The Danish theologian, Sören Kierkegaard, wrote about a wealthy woman who felt God calling her to the religious life. She felt she would be able to give up everything in order to do this, with one exception: she had a garden which was very important to her. It was a place for her to be alone, to be at peace and to renew herself. And she was unable and unwilling to give up the key to her secret garden.

There is an interesting symbol there for us. Each one of us has a secret garden and we are unwilling to give up the key to Jesus and to let him in.

35 *It's wrong to think that God really 'does' anything for us. Just as God doesn't give me anything – he offers it to me. When I say that God doesn't 'do' anything for me, he won't switch off the television so that we can say a family rosary, or the radio in the car so that I can pray.*

I heard of an old man whose beard went on fire and he prayed it would start raining! That's not how we should pray.

36 *I'm sure you've often heard the phrase, 'when the going gets tough, the tough gets going'.*

There's a story told about a college football game that turned out to be a terrible mismatch. One team outweighed the other by 30lbs per man, were more experienced and better coached etc. The lighter, weaker team was being terribly beaten, not only on the score board but also on their bodies. They were bruised, cut, bleeding and several first stringers already had left the game because of injuries. As they gathered in their huddle late in the final period, the quarter-back noticed that they had twelve men on the field, one more than the eleven allowed by the rules. That was all they needed! They would surely be in trouble if the referee noticed the extra man. He would award a penalty, thereby adding to their already deep humiliation. 'Look,' the quarter-back said to his team mates in a whisper, 'we'll try a running play that takes us past our bench. In the confusion, I want one of you to drop out. If you can do this quickly the referee may not notice and we can avoid the penalty at least.' With great confusion they succeeded in running the play right past the bench, but when they returned to the huddle to decide on their next play, the quarter-back discovered that six of his men had dropped out.

37 *We say that God's ways are not our ways.*

Supposing God had given us the job of arranging for his coming into the world, how do you think we'd go about working out the details? I've no doubt that we would form a committee and elect a chairman. Then the chairman would appoint various sub-committees, each of which would see to one particular aspect of the project. If we ran true to form, there would be a welcoming committee, a banquet committee, an entertainment committee, a publicity committee, a security committee and, God forgive us, there'd even be a ticket committee. The chairman might decide on a public relations committee, in charge of 'no hurt feelings', whose first order of business would be to make a survey – in the chairman's words, 'Let's give everyone an opportunity to be heard. For an affair like this, too much hassling wouldn't look good.' A questionnaire is printed, setting forth a number of key questions, beginning with, 'How shall we bring God into the world – in a spaceship, in an open limousine leading a motorcade of the world's dignatories, in solemn religious procession at one of the world's great shrines?'

But what about the possibility of God coming in an obscure dingey stable? Certainly no one on the committee would have thought of it.

38

I always insist that the Gospel is very simple, and this story would re-enforce that.

It's a story about an old missionary out in the mission fields who needed an assistant. They sent him a young scholar with a Ph.D. in theology. When he arrived the young man had to speak to the natives through the old man because he didn't know the language yet. In his first talk to these simple but wonderful people, the young man delved deep into his learning and said, 'Truth is absolute and relative. The gospel is absolute truth, but its application is relative to immediate needs.' Then he paused for a moment for the old missioner to translate this. The old missioner was seen to have a frown, a puzzle across his face, and then he arose and simply said, 'He says that he's awful glad to be with you.'

39

We always have to stress that Christianity is about service about doing good to others.

There is a great Japanese motion picture, regarded as the greatest film ever made. It is the story of an old man's struggle to attach meaning to his life after learning that he has cancer and only six months to live. This causes him to reflect on his uneventful life as a minor City Hall bureaucrat. The realisation that he has made no significant contribution to his fellow man troubles him spiritually. Despite his weakened condition, he resolves to do something for other people before he dies. With all his remaining energy, he gets behind a playground project which has had one obstacle after another thrown in its path by the local bureaucrats. As a result of his efforts, the playground is finally completed and the neighbourhood children are presented with their new paradise. The experience transforms the stuffy old ex-bureaucrat into a warm and compassionate human being. In the finale, the old man is seen contentedly seated on one of the new playground swings, slowly moving back and forth and softly humming a tune. There, peacefully, he dies.

The symbolism is clear. Only by rendering service to others with a warm and compassionate heart, only by assigning priority in human relations to 'what can I give?' over 'what can I get?' can we realise our potential as children of God. The childish posture of the old man on the children's swing, symbolises the childlike spirit which enables him to die in peace, and in hope.

---

40 A young man was shot to death in an underground gang war. He had a wonderful mother who was a very deeply religious woman. She had died when the boy was quite young and he had been cared for by the father, an alcoholic drifter. The boy grew up on the edges of the underworld and finally went to work for a gambling syndicate. Nobody knows exactly what happened but he was shot down in cold blood. The day of his funeral was cold and rainy. At the cemetery, those who came were almost ankle deep in mud. The clergyman did all he could to lend a morsel of dignity to the situation. The dead man's father was standing beside the grave with his hat in his hand. The funeral director moved to his side and quietly told him that it was time to leave. The father pushed him aside and said, 'I want to pray.' Then he knelt beside his son's open grave, with his hat in his hand, and he looked up, and in total agony said, 'My son, my son, your mother deserves something better of us than this.'

Anyone of us could look at our own lives at times and say, 'Jesus deserves something better than this from us.'

41 Imagine a scene like this: The great men of history are passing in front of God's throne. As Moses passes by, God says, 'What did you give to your people?' And Moses answers, 'I gave them the law.' And God replies, 'And what did they make of it?' 'Sin,' says Moses. Then Charlemagne passes by and God says, 'What did you give your people?' And he says, 'I gave them an Altar for the worship of the one true God.' 'And what did they make of it?' God asks. He replies, 'A stake for the burning of heretics.' Finally, Jesus passes in front of his father, who asks, 'What did you give your people?' Jesus replies, 'I gave them peace.' 'And what did they make of it?' 'War,' says Jesus.

42 There was a man one time who picked up the morning paper and, to his horror, he read his own obituary notice. The newspapers had reported the death of the wrong man. The caption read, 'Dynamite King dies.' The story identified him as a merchant of death. He was the inventor of dynamite and he had amassed a great fortune through the manufacture of weapons of destruction.

Moved by this disturbing experience, he radically changed his whole attitude and his commitment to life. A healing power, greater than the destructive force of dynamite, came over him. It was his moment of Pentecost. From them on, he devoted his full energy and money to works of peace and human betterment.

Today he is best remembered as the founder of the Nobel Peace Prize. His name was Alfred Nobel.

43 An old woman, living in Scotland, delighted in the sermons of a certain Scottish preacher. She had lived in an inexpensive basement apartment until she heard this man preach several times. Then she moved out of the dark basement apartment and into a sunny upstairs apartment. Because she had to sacrifice many things in order to live in the more expensive housing, a friend asked her why she had made the move. She replied, 'Oh! you can't hear that holy man preach and go on living in a basement.'

It wasn't the preacher of course, it was the Good Lord. It was the news, it was the message of the gospel shining through the preacher and into her life, that caused her to move out of the basement.

44 *The Bell of Amerhast* is a play in which the British actress, Julie Harris, played the role of the poet Emily Dickinson. In the first act the audience is made aware of Emily's religious problem. She came from a rigorous, rigid, puritan home in which her father was lord. Compulsory church attendance, compulsory daily prayer exercises etc. Then the spirit of rebellion came into the life of this very sensitive woman. She began to question some of the teachings and the customs she had grown up with. Yet she remained a deeply religious woman. Her poetry reveals a keen awareness of God's presence in the world and a deep consciousness of the great mystery of life and death. Emily Dickinson wrestled with doubts and fears about God and religion, as we all do from time to time. But there comes a point in the play where she says, 'I'm sure that no person will be truly happy until that person can say, "I love Christ."'

45 *In Matthew 25 we get the questions that will be asked on the last day. I remember coming across a version one time that went something like this:*
'I was hungry

and you said you need to build war machines so that you may be secure.

I was thirsty

and you said the world's resources are already stretched to their limits and it is time to get rid of the excess population.

I was a stranger

and you banded together because you trust only your own kind.

I was naked

and you said the poor we have with us always.

I was ill

and you said you were tired of misfits always complaining about the way things are.

I was in prison

and you said charity begins at home.

Lord when did we see you hungry or thirsty,

or a stranger or naked or ill or in prison?

The problem with Christianity is that Christians want to be committed to Christ without being committed to Christ's brothers and sisters.

---

46 *We always get the person who gets reformed, converted too much.*

There is the story of the changed man who asked, 'You stopped smoking because she asked you to?' 'Yes,' he answered. 'And you stopped drinking because she asked you to?' 'Yes,' he said proudly. 'And you stopped gambling because she asked you?' 'Yes.' 'And yet you've never married her?' 'Well, you see, after I had reformed like that, I found that I could do much better than marry her.'

---

47 A pastor once described his parish situation like this: Members of the parish: 2,546; Can't locate: 286; Left to work: 2360; Won't work: 540; Left to work: 1720; Too old: 318; Left to work: 1402; Too young: 555;

Left to work: 847; Sick and shut in: 88; Left to work: 759; Too busy: 390; Left to work: 369; Mad at someone: 92; Left to work: 277; Overworked: 275; Left to work: 2. Just you and me, and you better get busy. You can't expect me to do it all.

48 In an O'Henry story, called, *The Gift of the Magi*, the recently married Della and James Young are young and poor. So poor that neither has enough to buy the other a proper Christmas gift. In fact, weeks of scrimping and saving have netted Della only $1.87 for her gift offering. There are, however, things they possess and in which the Youngs take great pride. One is Jim's gold watch, that has been his father's and his grandfather's. The other is Della's hair, which reaches below the knees and might be the envy of any beauty queen. Out of Della's overpowering love for Jim emerges her solution to the gift problem. She cuts off her hair and sells it to a dealer. With the $20 realised, she buys a platinum watch fob-chain, an elegant replacement for the wornout strap presently attached to her husband's heirloom watch. Jim comes home and with fitting ceremony the gift is made. Jim too is prepared, with a gaily wrapped present for Della. Jim's gift is an elaborate set of combs for which she had always yearned, just the right shade for her now vanished hair. Then the final discovery, Jim had sold his watch to pay for the present. Della and Jim smiled contentedly. O'Henry concludes the story thus, 'Two foolish children who most unwisely sacrificed for each other the greatest treasures of their house. But in a last word to the wise, let it be said that of all who give gifts, these two are the wisest, of all who give and receive gifts, they are the wisest. Everywhere they are the wisest. They are the magi.'

49 There was a parish priest down in the south west of Ireland. He was a bit annoyed with these people on a Sunday morning who come in, kneeling with one knee on the cap at the back door, ready to make a bolt for the exit if you approach them with anything. So he decided to tidy up the act. He was going to bring in the commandos, the Redemptorists in the old days. They would spend the first few days of the mission sending you to hell and the next few days trying to get you back. But anyhow a whisper got round and the boys decided they were having none of it.

So on the opening night of the mission the missioner came out, complete with beretta, turnip watch, crucifix, wad of notes, (I mean sheets of sermon material), and there was one solitary man in the church. Your man, from out at the back of the mountain, hadn't been in town all week and he never heard about the boycott. So the priest didn't know what to do and he came down to your man to ask him, 'Now I'm supposed to preach a sermon here today and you're the only one that's here. What do you think I should do?' 'Ah, I wouldn't know the answer to them sort of questions at all, Father. I'm only a simple man. I live out at the back of the mountain there, but I'll tell you what, Father: I've got fourteen hens and when I go out in the morning to feed them ... when I call them, if only one of them comes ... I'll feed her, Father ...' 'Oh, fair enough ...' He got the message, so up he goes on the pulpit and began to feed the one solitary hen that came. An hour and half later he was still talking. He worked his way through from Adam and Eve to the second coming, and when he was finished he came to your man and he said, 'Well now, are ye happy enough with that?' 'Ah Father...I wouldn't know the answer to them sort of questions at all, but I'll tell you what, though: I've got fourteen hens and every day, Father, when I go out to feed them and if I call them and only one of them comes I'll feed her, Father, but I'm damned if I'll give her the whole bucket!'

50

I remember a young lad at home. I was amazed as a kid, because I knew he'd been left an awful lot of money but he still was going round, as we'd say at home, with no backside in his trousers. What I didn't understand was that he had to wait to come of age, which was twenty-one, and then he got the money. And of course, the neighbours could trace him back for generations past, and there was a bad drop some place, or his great granduncle on his mother's side was an alcoholic ... They were all watching to see what would happen. When your man came of age at twenty-one, he got the money and I'm not making much of a story of it when I say that I don't know what happened, because I never saw him since.

The point is that there is a coming of age for the inheritance of God's kingdom. It's not twenty-one. It mightn't even be ninety-one, or it simply could be seven. It really depends on you and me. Because the inheritance is ours when we are mature enough to claim it.

Sin and Forgiveness

51
I often say if God wanted a permissive society, he'd have given us ten suggestions and not ten commandments. But a sin is sin.
There's a story about two guys from my own part of the country, leaning up against the corner of a pub, waiting for it to open. As they were waiting for the pub to open, a funeral passed up the street. Now the local phrase is, 'Who's going up today?' 'Packie Murphy.' And your man says, 'Ah, is Packie dead?' 'He is,' says the other guy. 'What did he die of?' 'Well now, I don't rightly know,' he says, 'But whatever it was, I don't think it was anything very serious.'

52
It is in giving that we receive. We have often heard that, but we sometimes forget it. We are all of course sinners. We have a common vocation, the vocation to love, and therefore we have common sins: the failure to love.
One time there was a minister of religion. His business was bad or he lost courage or enthusiasm, and decided that he might be better off some other place. So he went off to look for a job and was very surprised, because he hadn't any reason to be in the job market before this, that he just couldn't get any other job. But there was a possibility of a job coming up at the local zoo. Unfortunately the actual job he applied for was not available just yet, but guess what happened! The local gorilla died – the great attraction for the children at all the school outings. They didn't have a replacement yet, so the minister was asked, would he mind getting into a gorilla costume. And he was just lying there, eating a few bananas, tumbling around the place, going in the back occasionally and coming out, and it didn't seem too bad of a job. As a matter of fact, he

got into the hang of it after a while. One day he got really excited about it, because he found that he was getting more attention now than he had been when he was in the pulpit. He jumped up on the trapeze this day and began to swing. And he really got carried away as he swung back and forth, much to the cheers of the children. The next thing, didn't he slip off the bar and he went flying in over a railing into another cage. And there was a tiger, standing over him. Forgetting that he was supposed to be a gorilla he shouted, 'Help! help!' and the tiger said, 'Shut up, you fool, I'm a minister too!'

Think about it. Whether you are dressed like a gorilla or a tiger, no matter what we are, in habit, roman collar or lying on skid row, we are all sinners anyhow. And the common leveller is that we are all equally dependent on the love and on the mercy of God.

53 I remember travelling by train from Monaghan to Dublin, as a kid. Sitting in the carriage, I was fascinated by the telegraph wires, as they would go 'zoom, zoom' out of sight, as they came to the next pole and to the next pole. And as I go on in life I often think of that image: that my life will tend to dip, to slide until something happens to give it a lift again and then here we go again ... and then something happens to give it a lift again. Whether it's the sacrament of reconciliation, or whether it's reconciliation with another person, or whether it is taking time out to pray to God, I will always need to make the effort, even if I fail.

Much worse than breaking the law of God is trying to keep it to the letter, because I am not able to. And only that God himself is carrying me, I'd be in trouble.

54 There was a lady walking through the park and she thought she heard somebody behind her. She got a little bit nervous. She walked faster and the footsteps behind her seemed to become faster as well. She quickened her step and, again, the step behind her seemed to quicken, and then she turned around and there was a young man behind her. And she said, 'Are you following me?' He said, 'I am.' And she said, 'Why are you following me?' And he replied, 'Because I am infatuated by you. I love you. I see you passing here every day. You are the most beautiful person I've ever seen. I love you so deeply.' He began to protest ever so vehemently. And she said, 'But if you look behind you, you'll see my younger sister and she is much more beautiful than I am.' And he turned around quickly and there was no one there. And he turned to her and said, 'You are only making a mockery, only fooling me.' And she said, 'If you were sincere in what you said to me, you would not have looked around to find my younger sister.'

Just think about that. Jesus is continually challenging us to make up our mind. He said, 'You are either for me or against me.'

55 There was a frog living in a forest in New Jersey, and he persuaded two geese to fly him down to Florida for the winter. He tied the end of a long cord to each of the geese and he held the centre of the cord in his mouth, and off they went. The journey was going well until someone on the ground noticed the strange sight passing by over head. 'Hi! look at that!' he shouted, 'That's fantastic! Whose idea was that, I wonder?' In his anxiety to get the credit for being so clever, the proud frog opened his mouth and shouted, 'Mine!'

56 In a famous cartoon, a man is seen with a very smug expression on his face. His wife is slightly turned away from him and is praying quietly, 'Dear God, please give Mr Perfect one tiny fault.'

57

The *New York Post* carried the story of a group of young people travelling by bus on a holiday trip to Fort Lauderdale in Florida. Not long after leaving, they noticed the dark-skinned, middle-aged man, poorly dressed, and looking quite worried as he sat slouched in his seat, head down. When the bus pulled in at a road-side cafe, everyone got out except Vingo, as the young people had named him. The young people were curious about him. Where had he come from? Where was he going? Finally, one of them sat next to him and said, 'We're going to Florida, would you like some of my Coke?' He took a swig and said than, 'Thank you.' After a while he told his story.

He'd been in a New York prison for four years. 'While I was away, I wrote to my wife and told her I'd be away for a long time, and if she couldn't take it, she should just forget about me. I told her not to write or nothing and she didn't. Not for three and a half years.' Then he said, 'She's a wonderful woman, really good, really something.' 'And now you're going home, not knowing what to expect?' the girl asked. 'Yes,' he replied, 'you see, last week when my parole came through, I wrote to her again. I told her I would be coming by on the bus. As you come into Jacksonville where we live, there's big oak tree. I told her that if she'd take me back, she could tie a yellow ribbon on the tree and I'd get off the bus and come home. If she didn't want me, forget it. No ribbon and I'd keep going.'

The girl told the others and soon they were all involved, looking at pictures of Vingo's wife and children and all getting more anxious and nervous as they approached Jacksonville. There was a hushed mood in the bus. Vingo's face tightened. Then suddenly all of the young people were up out of their seats, screaming and shouting, crying and dancing, all except Vingo. He just sat there stunned looking at the oak tree. It was covered with yellow ribbons, twenty or thirty of them. The oak tree had been turned into one big welcome banner. As the young people shouted, Vingo rose from his seat, made his way to the front of the bus, smiled back at his young friends through a flood of tears and got off.

No wonder a song was written about it. A song about the welcome for the prodigal when he arrives home. It would require very little change to turn this song into a hymn.

58 I remember speaking to a man sometime ago who had been very very interested in soccer. He was dying of cancer and the European Championships were on at the time. His married sons would bring him videos of all the games that had been on. He was fascinated by soccer and would watch video games on television for hours. At the end of the summer, after the European Championship, he was too weak now even to sit up in bed and I remember sitting with him one day talking and I said, 'Do you know what happens when you die?' Luckily enough he did not ask me how I knew, but he said, 'What?' So I said, 'The Lord sits you down and he puts on a video and it's called, *This is you life*. It's a very long video. You sit and watch this and you're not sure what you're going to see. Not just things that you remember but things you'd forgotten, and you're a little bit ill at ease. You're not sure what's going to come up. What actually happens is that there are blanks and then more and more blanks, and eventually it dawns on you that these were times when you did something wrong and you admitted it. God just pressed the erase button and wiped it out, because that's the kind of God he is. If you asked him what they were he couldn't tell you. When God forgives, he suffers from total amnesia and forgets. That's why I'm delighted that I'll be judged by God. I wouldn't trust people at all!'

59 Someone said one time that, when God forgives, he takes our sins and he dumps them into the deepest lake. Then he puts a sign on the lake which says, 'No Fishing' – leave them there, no going back.

60

Something that we can often forget in life is that, as the miles stretch ahead of you, the things that trip you up are inside in you.

A man one time stopped at the filling station and asked the guy at the filling station, 'What are the people like in this next village down the road?' Now this guy was being rather smart and didn't want to commit himself, so he asked, 'What were they like in that last village you came through?' 'Well, they were very friendly, and very nice.' And he said, 'Ah well, you'll find that these will be the same.' As it happened, the very next person who came to the filling station asked the very same question, 'What are the people like in this next village down the road?' And again the same reply, 'What were they like in that last one?' And he said, 'Oh, they were very dour and sour and unfriendly.' 'Ah, well, then,' says he, 'you'll find the people at the next village will be the same.'

61

At a religious revival meeting, 'the mourners bench' was the seat at the front of the church, and it was reserved for penitent sinners seeking forgiveness and salvation. There's the story of a pastor who regularly presided over revival meetings in the church that had no bell. It was his custom to assemble the congregation by mounting the high pulpit and blowing a huge fishhorn. One Sunday morning a pious soul, who regarded the preacher's mighty horn blast as offensive, sneaked into the vestry and filled the horn with washing-up liquid. Later, when the church was nearly filled, the pastor took to the pulpit to summon the stragglers. As he let go with the usual blast, the muffled sound that came from the horn was drowned out by shrieks from members of the congregation who had been sprayed with the soft sticky soap and the bubbles.

At a subsequent meeting the mourners' bench was crowded with penitents. One man seemed particularly distressed, moaning and calling on God for help. The horn-blowing pastor descended from the pulpit and bent over the troubled man. 'Tell me, Sir,' he said, 'What's your trouble? Let me help you with your probelm.' 'Oh, it's awful,' replied the man, 'It's so awful I can't tell you.' Gently the pastor said, 'If you will only unburden yourself, I know you'll feel better.' 'No, I can't!' came the answer, 'It's too awful.' 'Was it some lie you told?' said the pastor. 'No, worse than that!' said the man. 'Have you stolen?' 'No, worse than that.' The man's voice was trembling. The Pastor asked, 'Was it murder?' 'Oh, much worse than that,' the man replied. 'Ah, Ha!' said the Pastor, 'At last I have found the despicable creature who put soap in the horn for me!'

62 A woman went into a supermarket, collected her groceries and went into a coffee shop in the shopping complex. She had a cup of coffee and a kit-kat bar. She sat down at a table and put the bag of groceries beside her on the floor and began to sip her coffee.

There was a man across from her who started to open the kit-kat bar, take the wrapping off it and break a bit off. She was really annoyed with him! She grabbed it and broke a bit off it and began to eat it and said nothing. Eventually he reached over and took what was left of it and eat it and got up and walked away. This really infuriated her, because he had gone over to the counter and got another cup of coffee and this time he got a doughnut and sat at another table.

That was too much for her so she picked up her bag of groceries and, as she was passing his table, she just picked up the doughnut that he had and took a bite out of it and slammed it down in front of him and walked out.

As she was putting the groceries into the back of the car, she found there, on the top of her groceries, in her shopping bag, her bar of kit-kat!

There are many lessons to be learned from that.

63 There is a very beautiful old legend in which someone has pictured the last day – 'the day of the Lord' that the Bible talks about. In paradise on this last day everyone is celebrating, dancing and singing and shouting with great jubilation.

Everyone except Jesus. Jesus is standing very quietly in the shadows of the gates of paradise. Someone asks him what he's doing and, in the midst of all the celebration, he says, 'I am waiting here for Judas'.

That story symbolises the infinite quality of God's forgiving love which he offers even to Judas Iscariot. But the question remains, will Judas use his freedom to accept it or will he reject it? That is the question we must ask about the bit of Judas that's in all of us.

64 It's the day of judgment and a group of people are standing outside the gate of heaven, waiting for the gate to open, to walk in. They're delighted, they meet each other, they shake hands, they meet old friends; they were in the Legion of Mary together, they were on Parish councils and in confraternities; they are not surprised to see each other here, absolutely great and wonderful! The next thing, they hear a cheer in the distance. Someone asks, 'What's that?' They are told, 'He has forgiven the other ones as well!' 'What?' 'He has forgiven the other ones.' Well, they were furious! After all their trouble! After all their work, and here he is forgiving the other ones! And the next thing, a horn blows and somebody says, 'What's that?' They are told that it's the judgment. The judgment took place and they were still outside the gate.

65 A story is told of an old charwoman in London who was all hung up on her religious problems because she had lived a sinful life. She thought that God would never ever forgive her all these sins. She said to a

Christian evangelist, who was trying to convert her, 'But if he ever does forgive me he's never going to hear the end of it!'

66 In the novel, *Slaughterhouse Five*, there is an ex-prisoner-of-war who was an eyewitness to one of history's most devastating fire bombings. He cannot endure the real memory of the enormous human suffering caused by the massive air raid. Consequently he fantasises. He envisages a similar episode as a movie run backwards. Bombers, full of holes and corpses and wounded men, take off backwards from their home base and fly backwards towards the target area. Enemy fighter planes appear on the scene, flying backwards, bullets begin to be sucked out of the crewmen and their planes. Finally, still flying backwards, the bombers hover over the bombed area which is a large city; the bomb-bay doors are opened and exert a miraculous magnetism which shrinks the raging fires below, lifts the bomb fragments out of the debris and back into the planes' bellies, where they are re-assembled. Then, in backward flight, they are transported into their place of origin and there they are dismantled. The separate components are then buried in the ground by the people who had first assembled them, in the author's words, 'To hide them very cleverly so they would never hurt anybody again.'

That would be a wonderful prayer, wouldn't it? That we could undo the harm that we have done.

67 Late one night a cheerful truck driver pulled up to a roadside diner for some refreshments. As he was eating, three wild looking motorcyclists roared up to the diner's entrance. The atmosphere became tense as they stalked in wearing dirty leather jackets and swastika tatoos. Immediately they selected the truck driver as the target for their meanness. One poured salt and pepper on his head; another took his apple pie, placed it on the floor and squashed it under a dirty boot; the third upset his coffee, causing it to spill in his lap. The driver didn't say a word. He merely rose, walked slowly to the cashier, calmly paid his check and made his exit. 'That doode ain't much of a fighter,' sneered one of the invaders. The waiter behind the counter peered out into the night, then replied, 'He doesn't seem to be much of a driver either. He's just run his truck over three motorbikes.'

68 A woman in a prison in the States was leaning up against a wall chewing bubblegum, and I asked her, in a polite sort of way, 'What's a girl like you doing in a place like this?' And she said that she threw her baby out a third-story window in Philadelphia. She was as high as a kite on drugs, but I asked her why did she do that, and she said, 'He wouldn't stop crying.' And if you didn't know her, or understand her or her like, you would imagine she had no conscience whatever.

The next day, she came swaggering down the corridor, foul-mouthed language with the bubblegum, passing the other kids, walked into my room, slammed the door shut with her heel and now it was safe. And the bubblegum comes out of the mouth, goes into the basket, and she flops into a chair and begins to cry. She's guilty as hell. She's afraid of her life. She's homesick, but she dare not let the other girls outside see that.

I often think of Tina when I think of conversion or repentance, because all God is saying is, 'Will the real you please stand up?' Because the real you is a very good person.

Church

69 *I look around at today's world and wonder, 'where would you start?' I am always waiting for somebody else to change, the men of violence to stop. There has never been a bomb planted or a bullet fired that didn't begin in the* heart of a human person. It's not the world that's going to change; it's me and you. Let there be peace, and let it begin with me.

There was a man one time baby-sitting with his own kids but he obviously didn't have enough practice at it. It was a wet Saturday. With time and motion studies and running a business he would be excellent but dealing with his own kids was another story. They were getting on his nerves. But being inventive to some extent, he took down a magazine off a shelf and opened it up and tore out a map of the world. He cut it up with a scissors, jumbled it up to make a jig-saw, spread it out on the table and gave it to a seven-year-old lad to put together. He went on to give the second lad something to do. He was disgusted as well as amazed to look back very shortly afterwards and find that the first little lad was finished. He had all of the pieces of the jigsaw put together for the map of the world. Amazed more than anything else, he said, 'How did you do that?' And the young lad said, 'Well, you said that this was the world but I never saw one before and I didn't know where to start. But I turned over one of the pieces and there was a man on the other side, and when I put the man together the world was O.K.'

70 *Let me tell a story about a pig and a hen. It's one way of describing the Church that I grew up in and the church of now, because it is so vastly different. Jesus died to bring people across a bridge from a love of law into a* *law of love. Two thousand years later the Church had gone back over the bridge again into that love of law. And John XXIII, God love him, got on his knees and he said, 'Lord, would you ever give us another of them Pentecosts, because we blew that last one.' Now I believe that we are now living in the Acts of the Apostles of that second Pentecost. And the Church that I grew up in originally was a large homogenous sort of Church in which everybody did everything. No great deal! I defined such a Church one time as like the soccer cup final in Wembley where you had a hundred thousand people badly in need of a bit of exercise sitting down very comfortably critising twenty-two poor devils badly in need of a rest. But nowadays we are tying to get people down off the stands. You are the Church and the idea of vocation today in the Church is certainly way beyond a vocation to be a priest or a religious.*

The story is of a chicken and a pig out for a walk. You'll notice the pig is not too bright, he tends to repeat.

The chicken says: 'You know those people in that house down there?' 'Yeh, I do,' says the pig. 'They're very, very good people,' says the chicken. 'They are indeed,' says the pig. 'I must admit, they are. They're very good.' 'They're very good to us.' 'They are, yes, they are indeed.' Again you'll notice he's not too original. 'You know what I was thinking?' says the chicken. 'What were you thinking?' 'I was thinking we should do something for them.' 'A very good idea.' says the pig, 'I think we should do something for them. What did you have in mind?' 'I was thinking that we should give them something.' 'Good, good, that's a good idea,' says the pig, 'I think we should give them something. What did you have in mind?' 'I was thinking,' says the chicken, 'we should give them bacon and eggs.' And at that the pig stopped in his tracks and he said, 'No way! For you, that's only a little inconvenience, but for me it's a total commitment.'

Now in simple English, when I was a kid, the little inconvenience was O.K., but anything other than the total commitment today won't do. The men of violence and the men of the world are very committed and we cannot claim to be part of the solution if we're almost still part of the problem.

70

There was a priest one time who, because he was discouraged by the lack of response and the indifference in the parish, announced that the Church was dead and that next Sunday, if they wouldn't mind, they would have a funeral. So, of course, the word got around and they were very puzzled by it. The next Sunday they came and there was a coffin in the sanctuary with the lid to one side. And with a dead straight face, he invited the people to come up one by one to view the remains. And as they came up to look into the coffin to view the remains of the Church that was dead, the base of the coffin was a mirror and as each one looked in, you know what they saw? They saw the Church.

71

A row broke out between Amos and his people. Amos looked around and saw sanctuaries crowded with people who loved to worship. They loved the music, the preaching, the sacrifice, the praying. They enjoyed it. And then Amos looked at the world around them, and he saw poverty and racism, and he saw war and individual immorality and he saw the exploitation of people and Amos understood. In a very direct and blistering way, he said that unless the people's worship reflects the love and justice of God, and unless it results in the enhancement of love and justice in the world, not only is it ineffectual but it is also hated by God.

This is a very sobering thought. God may be rejecting this thing we pour so much of our lives into. This thing we love can turn sour and become destructive unless there is love and justice. This is precisely what Amos said to the people. Listen to the sobering words of God spoken through the prophet Amos some 2,800 years ago:

'I hate, I spurn your feasts! I take no pleasure in your solemnities, your cereal offerings! I will not accept nor consider your stall-fed peace offerings. Away with your noisy songs! I will not listen to the melodies of your harps! But if you would offer me holocausts, then let justice surge like water, and goodness like an unfailing stream.'

73 An angel asked the risen Jesus, on his arrival in heaven, 'Lord, who have you left behind to carry out the work?' And Jesus answered, 'A little band of men and women who love me.' 'But Lord, what if they fail when the trial comes, will all you have done be defeated?' 'Yes,' Jesus replied, 'if they fail, all I have done will be defeated.' The Angel persisted, 'Is there nothing more?' 'No.' said Jesus. 'What then Lord?' asked the worried angel. 'They will not be defeated. They will not fail,' was Jesus' answer.

74 *Every time I encounter a Christian community my hope is strengthened and renewed. And I often like to tell the following story.*
It is a story of a little child. It's supposed to have happened somewhere in South Dakota. The child wandered away from the house one night. It was dark and wet and dirty, and there was a door open and he was a little toddler ... He could have been gone for an hour or more before the mother missed him, and she went to get him and he wasn't there. She called his name, and no answer; she tried down in the basement; she tried upstairs; she searched every place. It took a long time to dawn on her that he just wasn't in the house. She ran down to the farmyard where the working men were finishing off after the day, and he hadn't gone there. As it happened, for miles in all directions, there were huge wheat fields. A search party was organised and it was dark and dirty and wet and late, and eventually they had to give up. And at dawn the next day, they were out again in force with extra help, and eventually one man just called everybody together and he said, 'This is crazy, crazy. We're running every whichway without any plan or organisation or attempt to work together. That child could be one or two yards away from you in that tall wheat and you wouldn't notice him. Why don't we just line up, hold hands, move in a straight line, and just take field by field?' So they held hands and walked down the first field, and about thirty

or forty yards down the field they found him. He had fallen into a gully; he was deeply unconscious; he'd been lying there since the previous night, with exposure and rain. They picked him up, rushed him back to the house, but it was too late, the last little spark of life was snuffed. And as they placed him in his mother's arms, and she sat on the doorstep with the people looking on, and the tears streaming down her face, she screamed from somewhere within the depths of her soul, and she said, 'In God's name, why didn't you people hold hands sooner?'

I look around this very country of my own and I say that again and again, to every group of Christians I meet. How many more people have to die? Why won't more of you people begin to hold hands before it's too late?

75

A Washington DC clergyman has written about a beautiful little town on the Coast of Maine called Kennebunkport. In the centre of Kennebunkport was a very New England-flavoured building that housed a bookstore called 'Kennebookport'. It was a most unusual bookstore. People came and sat on comfortable sofas and read the books without having to buy them. It was an incredible place. One could go there any time of the day or night, and just sit and read the books. If it was a chilly day, the proprietors would build a fire and serve hot cider to their guests. There was Martha, the cat, always around somewhere to enjoy being among the books and the people. People came from miles around to see the beautiful flowers growing along the steps leading up to Kennebookport. Many stores have signs that say, 'No bare feet', 'No children or pets', and so on, but the sign in front of Kennebookport said, 'Come on in. We love everybody. Welcome! We love icecream cones and kids and small dragons.'

At eleven o'clock one night, the fire sirens were heard by everyone in town. The Bookport burned down and was a total loss. Two days later, the people who had opened the Bookport published a little column in the local paper simply called, 'The Fire.' It began, 'We're licked; we give up; we've poured everything we have into this and now it is gone. These were our feelings as we huddled together in Docks Square last Friday night and watched the flames rip through our building. We clung to Fred and Tom, who have the store downstairs, and wept as the flames licked up the deck and lashed out of the windows of our little tower. But then something began to happen. Ruth made coffee. Chris went to our house to be with our kids. We watched these magnificent volunteer firemen as they fought with their hearts and souls to beat the flames and person after person came in to give us comfort. We were horrified when we heard that Walt had fallen from the roof and was seriously injured. At 2 a.m., as we struggled up the ladders into the smoking ruins to try to rescue what we could of our records, and finally stumbled home, although we were dazed and shattered, the seed of something was there and we didn't talk much about giving up. Then Saturday dawned. We went to the Square early and, as if by magic, people began to appear: men, women, teenagers, children, trucks, shovels, brooms. Still in a daze, we saw the twisted wreckage begin to disappear on its way to the dump. Lemonade, sandwiches and cakes apppeared and the work went on. We went home for a short break to find the flowers and the food and the cards and the letters and the gifts that were pouring into our house. People, some of them strangers, came to our door with sympathy. Businessmen came to offer space in their stores if we needed it. Chris once again took care of our kids all day. Then back to the Square where our dear Lonnie arrived at 2 o'clock to go to work and was so thunderstruck he couldn't speak. And the child who set up an offering pot for reflowering the Bookport deck and, perhaps most of all, the loving lady who stopped us in the street to say, 'The soul of our town has died, because the Bookport was our soul.' We wept and wept and wept again many times that day. But these were different tears. And slowly our hearts came alive again. We had come to the brink of despair, but the people of Kennebunkport called us back to our dream. Because of that, at the end of the day we hired a carpenter and began rebuilding the Bookport.

We are not Polyannas; we know that all is not bright. Walter Coubiac lies seriously injured in the hospital. We know that there will be little money and short rations for us for a long time now, and we know that Martha, our cat, will no longer doze on the gift books or curl up on the invoice box, because she suffocated in the fire. But we have learned that we will not be walking the road alone, because we have seen that Bookport is not ours: it belongs to the people of our town.

So although we don't have any books to advertise for a while, we'll share our pilgrimage with you each week in this newspaper space. The fire took all the things we had, it burned hot enough to destroy our books, to turn our flowers into scorched stumps and to kill our cat, but that same fire burned bright enough to light up our dream once again and to show us the faces and the hearts of the people of our town, and in that light we are building again.'

This is a simple but apt illustration on making the connection between love of God and love of neighbour.

76

We have always been taught that the power of the Eucharist is infinite – but do we believe it? If I were asked to say an anniversary Mass for someone, the family could get quite upset if I offered the same Mass for someone else as well.

There was a mother who had twin babies who were delicate. The doctor suggested that, as the weather was really beautiful, she should ensure that they got one hour's sunshine everyday. Nothing was too good for her children, so she put the first little boy out in the garden from noon until 1.00pm; then she put the little girl out from 1.00pm until 2.00pm. She couldn't put the two out at the same time, because she wanted each to get the full benefit of the sun!

I imagine that God smiles more often than cries when he looks at us – because we're often more stupid than evil!

Truth

77 It was the Christmas pageant and the Nativity play. And one lad had one simple job to do: he was the Inn Keeper and he was to stand at the side of the stage and tell Mary and Joseph there was no room and that they were to go away.

They had rehearsed this and practised it and on the night Mary and Joseph came along, and, begolly, your man took them by the hand and brought the two of them in! And then he began to cry because he was going to get scolded for not doing what he was told. But in his heart and soul he couldn't say there was no room because there was plenty.

And, after all, St Joseph was a cousin of his!

78 I heard a story recently about a meeting in hell where the daddy devil was very upset with all these renewal programmes. You know, Christian family movements and Charismatic renewal and Medjugorje groups, prayer groups and God knows what all. If things are allowed go on like this, sure we'll be out of business after a while. So he wanted them to really get a move on, and he called them all back to base to think, think, think. He wanted a plan for the nineties, up to the year 2,000.

After a while, one little devil put up his hand and he said he thought he had an idea. All of his pals cheered him on and the daddy devil asked him what it was. He said, 'Why don't we tell them that there is no such place as hell at all, that there is a heaven alright but no such place as hell, and then they'd say, "Ah, well, sure it doesn't matter. You can do whatever you like, you're not going to go to hell anyhow."' And all his pals cheered, but the auld fella, the daddy devil, wiser in his ways, thought for a while and he said, 'No, no, no. You don't understand the human species. You don't understand, because they would never, ever believe that. From the time when they are children, they know when they do wrong. Even a dog looks guilty when he does something wrong. They're even punished by their sins. They would never believe that.'

So, much deflated, the young devil sat back down again and the daddy devil ranted and raved and told them to come on and put on their thinking caps. And eventually another devil stood up and said, 'How about this one?' 'What is it?' 'Supposing we tell them that there is a hell but there's no such place as heaven. Then of course they'll say, well, what's the use in trying? We're all going to end up in hell anyhow. It doesn't make any difference.' And all of his pals cheered and thought it was a great idea. But the daddy devil thought for a while and shook his head and said, 'No, no, no. It just shows you don't understand the human species. They would never believe that. There is some sort of a resilience in them that, even when today is lousey, they somehow expect that tomorrow will be better. That's the way they go. I never can understand it but somehow there is something in them, that is put there by God, that gives them hope for a better tomorrow. No, that wouldn't do.'

So at this stage he was really hopping mad and ranting and raving and eventually this devil stood up and said, 'I think I have it!' And he said, 'What's that?' 'We'll go up and we'll tell them that there is a hell and that there is a heaven but there's no hurry. Take your time! There's no urgency!' And the daddy devil stepped down off his throne and shook hands with him and he said, 'Listen, boys, get back up there at once and get that message out right, left and centre. Let them believe in heaven if they want to; let them believe in hell if they want to; but if you can convince them that there is no hurry, there is no urgency, then we are back in business.'

Have you heard that whisper at any time?

79 In a particular village there was a wise old man who was looked upon as a sage. People came to him for advice and words of wisdom and he was looked up to. And there was a young lad in the village who had an opportunity of going away for education. He came back, considered to be very intelligent and of great book-learning. He was jealous of the old man with his wisdom. So he decided to show him up a bit and test him. He decided he'd get a small bird – we'll say a robin – he would hold the robin in his hand, with some feathers sticking out at one end and a beak at the other, and he decided that he would come to the old man and firstly ask him, 'Is this a bird?' Then he would ask him, 'Is the bird alive or dead?' If the old man said, 'He's dead,' the young man would open his hand and let the bird fly away. If the old man said, 'The bird is alive,' the young man would just crush the bird in his hand and hand it to the him dead. In other words, he was going to catch him out. So he came along and said, 'Now, I have a poser for you here. Is this a bird? What do you think?' The wise man said, 'Yes, it seems to be a bird.' Now the next question: 'Is this bird alive or is it dead?' And the old man put his hand on the young lad's shoulder and said, 'That, my friend, depends totally on you.'

80 In a Charlie Brown comic strip, Linus comes up to Charlie and says, 'Charlie Brown, do you want to know what's the trouble with you?' Charlie Brown says, 'No.' In the third panel they just stare at each other, and then Linus says, 'The trouble with you, Charlie Brown, is that you don't want to know what's the trouble with you.'

81 *There is always a great danger in fundamentalism.*
I heard of a guy who just opened the Bible to get some direction for the day, and his eyes fell on the statement, 'And Judas went out and hanged himself.'

82

There is the story about the horse trader in the hills of West Virginia. He was a sharp dealer but he always justified his horse trading by quoting the Bible. He knew just what passage to use in every case. On one occasion he had a very sick horse on his hands. He tried to sell it but everyone in the area knew the horse was sick and they wouldn't touch it. Then a stranger came along and it wasn't long before he was riding out of town on the sick horse, as the horse trader counted a thick wad of notes. This upset the horse trader's wife very much. 'Don't tell me you sold that sick horse to someone?' 'Yea,' he said, 'a preacher passed through and I sold him the horse.' 'Really! A man of the cloth!' she said. 'Oh, it's all right,' he replied, 'As the Bible says, he was a stranger and I took him in!'

83

A young man was filling in a application for admission for the University of Wisconsin. In reply to a request to list 'your personal strengths', he wrote, 'Sometimes I am trustworthy, loyal, helpful, friendly, courteous, kind, obedient, cheerful, thrifty, brave, clean, reverent.'

Further down the form he had to write under the heading, 'List your weaknesses'. He wrote, 'Sometimes I am not trustworthy, loyal, helpful, friendly, courteous, kind, obedient, thrifty, brave, clean and reverent'.

84

Externally, we can be seen to do something and yet conversion, or 'yes' to God, is not what is going on in the heart.

There was a little girl who'd been misbehaving and really giving her mother a rough time. The mother told her to go sit in the corner until her father came home, at which time they would discuss the whole situation. The little girl went over and stood in the corner. She went that far, but she refused to sit, another symbol of her rebellion. After another hassle, the mother literally forced the child to sit down. When the father came in, he asked the little girl what she was doing and she said, 'Well, on the outside I'm sitting down but inside I'm still standing.'

85 During World War 11, the German government distributed to the people radio sets that would receive only the official Nazi stations, thus preventing them from hearing other versions of reality.

Like single station radio sets, many of us are only tuned to divine transmissions for blessings and comforting experiences. If we are not receiving the complete transmission, it is not because God is not sending the signals; it is because we are practising selective tuning, which lets in the message of comfort and security and shuts out the message of challenge and of commitment.

86 In a certain town, a local bank was trying to help married students with their financial problems. They hired as many male students' wives as possible, because it was a University town. But their problem arose when the wives became pregnant and they would stay on the job longer than the bank officials preferred. So eventually the bank adopted a rule that required the pregnant wives periodically to stand against a wall, and when the time came that any part of their anatomy bumped the wall, they would have to leave their jobs.

One of the wives was so incensed at this indignity that she went to the national labour relations board and she claimed unfair discriminatory tactics. The board agreed with her and ruled that this same test would have to be applied equally to all employees.

As a result the bank lost two students' wives and three male vice-presidents.

The rules apply to all!

87　We can find it difficult to allow people be what they are. Bonhoeffer was executed by the Nazis for refusing to submit to Hitler's tyranny. One of his close friends has written about an experience he had with Bonhoeffer one Sunday as they walked home from church together.

They were talking about the Service and the sermon and so on, when suddenly Bonhoeffer's friend told him that there was something about him that he found very upsetting. 'There are times when you seem distant and cold,' he said, 'Sometimes it's hard to get close to you; sometimes you seem unresponsive and you make people feel uncomfortable.' Suddenly Bonhoeffer stopped the man short by exclaiming, 'Why can't you let somebody be who he is?'

88　We all know people who easily take offence at some word or comment that was not intended to be hurtful at all.

A woman was driving round a hairpin bend on a narrow country road and she swung a bit wide and forced a man coming in the opposite direction to swerve sharply to avoid collision. To add insult to injury, or so it seemed, as the woman passed by the man, she cried out, 'Pig!' Hastily categorising her as a ignoramus, he shouted back, 'Jackass!'

As he rounded the curve, he crashed into the biggest pig that ever was seen.

89　In *The Fiddler on the Roof*, Tevier, the leading character, is a pious Russian Jewish peasant. He loves to stare up at the sky and argue with God. In one particularly dark moment, and indeed we all have these, when everything seems to be going wrong in his little Jewish community, Tevier looks towards the sky and says to God, 'It's true that we are the chosen people, but once in a while can't you choose someone else?'

90

And then there's the story of the seminarians' instructor who gave a theology course which, year after year, was regarded by the students as being a snip, just an easy number. This was because each time the instructor gave the same, one-question examination, 'Discuss the trials and tribulations of Job.' Obviously the students, knowing what was coming, were well prepared. One time, however, the instructor surprised them. He changed the question and only one student passed the course. The new question had read, 'Criticise the Sermon on the Mount.' When the one student who passed was asked how he did it, when everyone else failed, 'I answered the question as follows: "Far it be from me to critise Our Lord. However, there are a few things I would like to say about the trials and tribulations of Job."'

91

In the novel, *Dearly Beloved*, by Anne Morrow Lindberg, there's a moving passage in which Deborah, the mother, is adjusting the wedding veil for Sally, her daughter. They have lived in the same house for twenty years but never really enjoyed deep sharing or real communication. The mother is feeling this deeply now on the wedding day. With great feeling, Anne Morrow Lindberg describes the scene.

Deborah went to her daughter, kissed her lightly on the forehead and hesitated for a moment, looking urgently, almost pleadingly, into her wide eyes. Wasn't there something she could say at this moment, mother to daughter, something real? Sally too seemed to be pleading, asking for confirmation. 'Your father will be up in a moment,' Deborah blurted in a rush. That was all she could say. The words for something deeper never came, the real thing was never said.

That is a commentary on life for so many of us, in marriage, in the family, with friends and with others. We go places and do things together, but the real thing never gets said; the real communication never takes place.

92

I remember as kid there was one great 'put-down' line: when you said to someone, 'Oh, you think you're great!'

I remember reading one time about a political leader in Washington DC who was in his living room one evening. He turned to his wife and said, 'My dear, do you know how many truly great men there are in the world today?'

Unhesitatingly she replied, 'No, I don't, but I do know there is one less than you think there is.'

Many of us have this problem, of being ego-centred, and as a result we could quite often end up hurting people.

93

A man had two sons. As the first son was leaving home, he asked his father what he should expect life to be. The father said that life was a wonderful adventure, people were basically very good, and there would be much joy, love and happiness along the way.

When the second son was leaving home, he asked his father the same question. 'Life is rough and tough,' his father told him, 'and you will meet many selfish and unfriendly people; and you will have to fight and struggle to survive.'

Both lads found out exactly as the father said. They each found what they had expected to find.

Faith/Trust

94

Jesus said, 'The sin of this world is unbelief in me.' – You don't believe me.' He came to tell us about the Father's love. He came to tell us about the birds of the air, the lilies of the field or why be like the heathen? He came to tell us about the Father's love and to assure us of our daily bread.

There was an Indian lad one time, who, on his thirteenth birthday, was taken out into the jungle. It was a test of his courage before he would be accepted into full membership of the tribe. He was going to be left on his own, in the jungle all night, to see how he'd do. He'd a very long night. He never thought the night could be this long! Every leaf that fell, every branch that squeeked, every sound from the undergrowth, terrified him. But he couldn't very well run – where do you run to in a jungle in the dark? There's no way he could sleep. He never, ever thought a night could be this long. He thought morning would never come. He hung in there, and eventually, as happens, morning did come and his eyes became accustomed to the dawn and the light and, as he looked around, he was amazed to find, standing right behind a tree, right near to him, his father. He had been on duty all night with a gun, on guard. And his first reaction was, well if I had known that he was there, I'd have slept soundly all night.

95

There was a family one time which became very impoverished. The family business failed. The neighbours, being good neighbours, wanted to know could they help. And the father said, 'I'll tell you what, I'd give anything to be able to take my wife and kids and get away out of this place and start all over again.' So the neighbours said that they would see what they could do. And they eventually came up with money and presented them with tickets for a fourteen day voyage on the high seas to New York. Now the family had no idea how you could possibly prepare for such a voyage, so they got cheese and lettuce and they made sandwiches, filled boxes of sandwiches, got into the boat, got into a cabin by themselves, a frightened parochial group. On the first, second, third, fourth, fifth, sixth, and seventh day, when they were hungry they ate sandwiches. They didn't have anything else. On the eighth, ninth, tenth day you couldn't even mention the word sandwiches, and now they were so sick! With a day or two to go before arriving in New York, one little lad begged his Mam and Dad for a penny or two, so he could go up on top and buy a sweet or something. So they gave him a penny or two and off he went. An hour later he hadn't come back. The father was very worried. He had no choice, he had to go up on top and look around. He was horrified! There were rows and rows of tables and all these people sitting around the tables and his son right in the middle of them. And they were all eating a big meal – chicken, potatoes, vegetables, ham, a big tumbler of orange juice. The young lad was stuffing himself goodo! The father came up behind him and said, 'Why did you do this? You know I can't afford this! Why did you do this?' And the young lad's eyes lit up and he said, 'Daddy, guess what? We could have had this all the time. This was included with the tickets.'

Jesus could say, 'But look, I promised you this all the time. I spoke to you about abundant life, about joy pressed down and flowing over, about my peace. For some reason or other you settled for sandwiches! I never ever intended that and you certainly didn't get that idea from me.'

96 *Thinking in terms of trusting God, I remember a programme I saw out in the Mid-West years ago.*
Three people are given three trollies in a supermarket. The whistle blows and they go charging down the

isles and grabbing stuff off shelves as fast as they can. They are being timed by a stopwatch and when the whistle goes, they are to be at the checkout. Each basket is checked out and the person with the greatest amount of goods is the winner.

At the checkout, as you could imagine, one is taking a little peep into somebody else's basket and saying, 'I'm sorry I didn't take three of those.' In other words, no matter what you did you'd see something at that checkout to make you say, 'Why didn't I do this?'

Anyhow, bring the three of them back again and put in somebody else, only this person is a Christian as I understand a Christian. The whistle goes. They go charging down the isle and here's your man, smiling to himself because if you're saved you're supposed to look saved. So he picked up a loaf of bread and put it in his trolley, and some woman let something fall, so he picked it up and put it into the trolley for her. He went on down a little bit further and he got a pound of butter and put it in with the bread and he arrived down at the checkout with the others and immediately he found himself being stared at with utter disbelief, utter scorn, as if to say, 'Who let you out?' And one of the women just couldn't take this anymore and she really berated him, 'Did anybody tell you what this thing is all about? I mean, what's wrong with you?' And he smiled said, 'My father owns the supermarket.'

You see, if I really take Jesus seriously, I'll come back tomorrow for what I need for tomorrow, that's all.

97

There were little twin boys in a mother's womb and after a while they became aware of each other and they became aware of the cord. They decided, as they were chatting among themselves, that their mother must love them very much because she was sharing her very own life with them. After a while they became aware of some changes in themselves, like little nails coming etc., and they asked themselves, 'What's this ... what's happening?' And one of them said, 'We're going to be born.' The other one said, 'Born! I don't want to be born, I want to stay where I am.' 'Well, you can't stay where you are, you have to be born.' 'Ah, I don't want to! How do you know there's any life after this? Did you ever see anybody who was ever born?' The other one says, 'No, but there, there must be ...' And the first one said, 'How do you know there's a mother anyhow ... I bet you we only invented her for our own security.' And here you have the two of them arguing. One of them is already a little atheist and the other guy is a man of faith. Which in simple English means, he has proof of nothing. For if you had the proof you wouldn't need faith.

So, eventually, they know it's time, it's safe and they are born. And they open their eyes, and they look at each other, and they look up at the face of their mother, and then they look at each other again, as if to say, 'Weren't we foolish? Surely this is something marvellous, and we could never have understood this!'

---

98 A man came out from a supermarket and saw that the side of his car had been badly dented. He was only somewhat relieved when he saw a note under the blade on the windscreen. And he picked up the note and read, 'Dear sir, I have just bumped into the side of your car. The people who saw me do this are still watching, and they believe that I am now leaving my name and address on this piece of paper. But they are wrong.'

Similarly, I could visit somebody in a hospital because I feel sorry for him or I could visit him because I want to see that guy suffering.

---

99 There was a man one time who insisted that when he asked God for something, God was going to give it to him. The dam had flooded and broken its banks and there was a tidal wave on its way down into the village. The police came by with sirens, calling on the people to get out of the house, get out, move quickly, the floods are coming! But this man ignored the call. Why? Because he asked God to help him. Then the floods came roaring down and burst his front door and he went upstairs and out on the windowsill. Somebody came along with a boat and asked him to get in. Oh no, he wouldn't. He trusted God. God was going to look after him. And of course, the floods rose higher and he climbed up on the roof, and when he was on the roof a helicopter came along and lowered a winch for him to grab. No, he refused. God was going to look after him. And of course the guy was drowned.

He arrived up to the gates of heaven and he was very annoyed. Peter realised there was something wrong with him. 'You're grumpy, what's wrong with you?' 'What's wrong? I prayed. I asked God to save me and, after all my trouble, I wasn't answered and I drowned.' And Peter said, 'We did send you the police didn't we? And somebody in a boat, and then we sent somebody to you with a helicopter! Surely we did answer your prayers?'

100

A traveller boarded a train in New York city. Immediately he went to the porter and said, 'Look, I want to get off in Washington DC but once I'm asleep it's very difficult to waken me. Sometimes I say nasty things I don't really mean. Here are a few dollars, please, no matter what I say, don't be offended, just wake me up and put me off the train in Washington!' Hours later, he awakened as the train pulled into the station at Richmond, Virginia, a hundred miles past Washington where he had intended getting off. The man was furious. He found the porter and angrily denounced him for his incompetence. Later the conductor asked the porter, 'What happened? I've never seen anybody as mad as that fella who got off in Richmond!' To which the porter replied, 'That's nothing, you should have seen the anger of the fella I put off the train in Washington!'

101

Jesus said, 'The sin of this world is unbelief in me.' And faith, I've said before, is in my feet, not in my head. I remember seeing this in action in a very simple way some years ago.

There was this young girl of eleven, dying of leukemia. Her Dad came with her to a Dublin hospital and stayed with her day after day, week after week. There was nothing that he wouldn't do for her. I would never have to tell her that her Daddy loved her. She could see that for herself every day.

Then, because she knew and was convinced that her Daddy loved her, she trusted him totally. Because that's all faith is. Faith is a response to love. Because she trusted her Daddy totally she obeyed him completely, because he would never ever ask her to do anything that was not for her good. And because she trusted him, she was not afraid, because he was there and she knew he was still going to be there tomorrow.

That represented in simple fashion, what I think God's original plan was. When that plan got messed up, God said, 'Look, I'm going to give you a Spirit of truth, who will bring you back out of those lies, back into truth and back to the garden. Back to the hug of the Father who's waiting for you.' Satan is a liar, the father of lies.

102

A young man is making a difficult mountain climb. As he inches his way up the steep granite face, he loses his hold and begins to slip. Frantically, he grabs a frail stem lodged in a crevice. If he loses his grip, he'll fall thousands of feet to certain death.

In his panic, he looks up and shouts, 'Oh! God! If you are up there, help me now!' So the voice of God says, 'If you want me to help you, you must have faith.' 'I have faith God, lots of faith, but please help me quickly!' Then God says, 'Have faith, let go of the branch and you will glide gently to earth there below.' After a short consideration, the young man shouts, 'Is there anyone else up there?'

103

I'm often amused at the gospel story about Dives the rich man. When Dives was in hell, he wanted God to let him go back and tell his brother that he'd better change his ways. And according to the story, the reply was, 'If they didn't believe the prophets, they certainly are not going to believe someone who came back from the dead.' Later on, Jesus himself would come back and people wouldn't believe him either.

There was a patient in a psychiatric hospital in Boston. He was convinced that he was dead. That was his fixation. He was convinced that he was a corpse. The doctors tried to reason with him. Finally, they succeeded in obtaining his agreement to the proposition that corpses do not bleed, and he agreed to allow the doctors to conduct a little test based on that proposition. The doctors proceeded with the test by pricking the man's finger causing the blood to come. The patient looked at his finger for a moment and then said, 'Well, what do ye know, so corpses do bleed!'

104

There is the story about three clergymen: a Jewish Rabbi, a Protestant minister and a Roman Catholic priest. They were fishing together. They rowed to the middle of a small lake and cast their lines. Soon they ran out of bait. The rabbi volunteered to go for more. Calmly he stepped off the boat and walked across the water to the shore. When he returned in the same manner, it was discovered that they trio's canteens were empty. Immediately the minister collected them and, like the rabbi, walked across the water to the shore and filled them up and returned. Later when the men grew hungry, they realised they had forgotten a lunch basket, whereupon the priest quickly rose, stepped off the boat and immediately plunged to the bottom of the lake. When he had surfaced, he heard the rabbi say to the minister, 'I suppose we really should have told him where the stones are.'

105 *In my own life, any compassion I have, any empathy I have, has come from my own brokenness. There is no other way to get it. And any worthwhile growing in my life has always been at times of conflict. We can take a lesson from nature in this area.*

We have all seen cocoons hanging from trees and bushes in the springtime. The cocoon is protection for our wormy creature, in the process of maturing into a butterfly. The grace of the butterfly is really beautiful to behold, but full maturity does not come without a struggle. Biologists have discovered that the struggle to break through the cocoon of old life into new life is absolutely necessary for the butterfly's survival. Without the struggle, the tiny wing muscles would not develop the strength to fly and the butterfly would die in the cocoon.

106 In A.J. Cronin's bestselling novel, *The Keys of the Kingdom*, there is a young doctor who simply can't believe in God. But he is a sensitive, compassionate person and he goes to China to help the victims of famine and plague. Eventually, the doctor himself is stricken. Even on his deathbed he remains an unbeliever. 'Funny', he says to a priest friend, 'I still can't believe in God.' And he answers, 'Does that matter now? God believes in you.'

107 A rigid old so-and-so sought advice from a Marriage counsellor. 'I hate my husband. He's making my life miserable. I want a divorce and I want to make things as tough as possible for him.' The counsellor advised, 'Begin by showering him with compliments, indulge him in every whim. Then when he realises how much he needs you and wants you, start your divorce proceedings.' Six months later, the counsellor met the woman and asked, 'When are you going to file your divorce papers?' 'Are you out of your mind?' replied the woman indignantly, 'We're divinely happy.'

Hope

108 *A Chinese proverb says, 'If you hit flea on head of dog with sharp edge of sword, you injure dog more than flea' Quite often the cure is more dangerous than the disease.*

A policeman was called on to talk a man down who was out on a bridge about to jump into the river. As the pooliceman approached him, he eventually got his attention sufficiently to agree that, 'If I give you ten minutes to tell me what's wrong with this world, then you must give me ten minutes to tell you what's right with this world, and why I think you shouldn't jump.' So they agreed to that.

The man began and he could have gone on for an hour about what's wrong with the world. And the policeman stopped him and he said, 'Your time is up.' So the policeman began to tell him what was right with this world and why he shouldn't jump. After two or three minutes, he ran out of things to say, and he just reached over, took your man by the hand and the two of them jumped.

109 *The ultimate sin for a Christian is despair. When Judas took the morsel, Satan entered into him and therefore Judas despaired. Peter committed the same sin on the same night but he knew that Jesus stilled loved him.*

There were two little lads, one of them was a pessimist and the other was an optimist. So they put the pessimist into a room full of toys and closed the door. They took the optimist and they put him into a room across the corridor, full of manure from the farmyard. An hour later they came back to see how they were doing and they looked into the pessimist with the room full of toys. He was sitting on the floor in the middle of all the toys and he was crying, because there was no drum. He found something missing. They went across the corridor to the optimist with the room full of manure from the farmyard, and he didn't even hear them opening the door. The eyes were popping out of his head with excitement and he had a little shovel. 'What are you doing?' And he said, 'Quiet! With all this manure there's got to be a pony here somewhere!'

110

God invites me and that's all he does. Satan bullies me - ask the alcoholic, ask the compulsive gambler, ask the kleptomaniac.

There was a guy one time who was working for a slave-driver who treated him like dirt, who would burden him with guilt and scolding and discouragement. One day a man came in to work in the place and saw him and thought he was worth more than that. So he asked him to come and work for him. This new man gave him responsibility, gave him respect, and gave him many, many opportunities for encouraging and affirming and confirming others.

One day his former employer comes in and he begins to rant and rave and scold and give out and find fault and bully. Now what do you think he'll do? He'll go to the door, open the door and tell this guy, 'Listen, I owe you nothing anymore, get out at once.'

That's what Jesus says, 'I give you full authority over all the power of the evil one.'

111

Waiting for Godot is a drama in which Samuel Beckett offers a very pessimistic view of the human condition. The action centres around two tramps who wait in vain for a person named Godot. Godot, obviously, is the author's symbolic name for God. Throughout the play, the tramps keep talking about his coming, but Godot does not come. When the final curtain comes down, the audience knows that Godot will not come, ever.

'We are waiting in vain,' is the theme of the play. But Christians are otherwise persuaded. With the first disciples at Resurrection time, with the New Testament authors, with the early Christian church, and with the followers of Christ down through the ages, we sing, 'Alleluia, Godot has come.' We cry out, 'Emmanuel! God is with us.'

112

In A.J.Cronin's novel, *The Keys of the Kingdom*, one of the main characters is Father Chisholm. He is a missionary priest who has worked almost all of his life in China against overwhelming odds. There is a passage in which this good Christian missionary gives a clue to his remarkable courage and hope. He is talking to a distressed friend, a native farmer who is wringing his hands and bitterly complaining because his garden has been completely washed out by a seasonal flood. 'My plantings are all lost,' he cries, 'We shall have to begin all over again.' And Fr Chisholm replies quietly, 'But that's life my friend, to begin again when everything is lost.'

113

Sometimes we pray for something and we don't get it, and sometimes we set limits to what God can do for us. Sometimes we encounter that God of surprises who does so much more than we ever hoped for.

A farmer one time ordered a dozen chickens from his poultry dealer. 'I'll be away all day,' he advised the merchant, 'so just leave them on my front porch.' When he returned home that evening, the farmer found only an empty crate, with a faulty latch, on his porch. Immediately the man set out in a frantic search of the countryside. Next morning, he called the dealer to complain. 'Look here,' he said, 'because of your negligence, I spent half the night looking for those lost chickens. It took me four hours to find all twelve.' The dealer replied, 'Twelve! You've done well my friend. I thought you ordered half a dozen. There were only six chickens in that crate that I left!'

75

114

Writing to the Corinthians, Paul says, 'All things work together for good'.

An old man and his only son live together in a small rural community. One night the old man's horse wanders off and his neighbours come to express their sympathy over the horse. The old man says to them, 'How do you know that it's ill fortune?' A few days later, the horse returns followed by an entire herd of wild horses. Now the neigbours come to congratulate the old man on his good luck, but the old man says, 'How do you know that this is good fortune?' Time passes, and the son takes to riding the wild horses, until one of them throws him and breaks his leg. Again the neighbours come to express sorrow for the old man's bad luck. 'How do you know it's bad luck?' asks the old man. A short time later, a Chinese warlord comes into the town to recruit all the able-bodied young men for his next war. But the son escapes the draft because of his broken leg. Once more the neighbours tell the old man how pleased they are at his good fortune. Here the story ends, but obviously it could go on and on.

115

The guy at the pool for thirty-eight years is asked by Jesus, 'Do you want to be healed?' There are people who would say, 'Don't straighten me out. I'm enjoying my confusion.' Your man could have lived to regret having no excuse for not working.

There is the story of a man who was very unhappy to be discharged by his psychiatrist after years of analysis. 'You're cured.' said the doctor. 'Some cure!' the man snorted, 'When I came here I was Napoleon Bonaparte. Now I'm nobody!'

116

Franz Kafka wrote the parable called, *An Imperial Message.* In it he asks you, the reader, to imagine that the emperor of your country is dying. He has an earth-shaking message to leave before he dies and he decides to send it to you only. He sends a messenger who immediately encounters formidable obstacles on the way. Enormous crowds of people are obstructing his journey. The messenger struggles mightily but is unable even to break out of the central rooms of the emperor's palace. If only he could get out of these rooms. Even so, if and when he does, there will still be the stairs to manoeuvre, the palace courts to cross. Still another palace to pass through, then more stairs and more courts. In a thousand years, no one could make his way through that maze of confusion. Meanwhile you are sitting at your window each evening waiting and dreaming dreams about the messenger's coming. 'That,' says Kafka, 'is our lot, to sit and wait and dream about a messenger who never arrives.'

I use that story because for us Christians, the messenger has come. The messenger has broken through. After thousands of years, the messenger, Jesus Christ, is at your window at this very moment with a life and death message to deliver.

117

Marguerite Higgins covered the Korean war and she received the Pulziter Prize for her perceptive, sensitive stories. On one occasion she wrote about being with the Fifth Company of Marines. It was early evening and the company had stopped the march to have supper. The men were experiencing bone-deep fatigue, anxiety, fear. One marine was leaning back against a truck eating his cold meal from a tin can. He'd been in the field for many days and his clothes were stiff with dirt and cold. His heavily bearded face, encrusted with mud, was almost expressionless because of an immense fatigue. One correspondent, in the small group of reporters who were on the scene, asked that marine a strange and perhaps insensitive question, 'If I were God and could grant you anything you wanted, what would you want most?' The marine stood motionless for a few minutes. Then he looked up at the reporter and said, 'Just give me tomorrow, please.'

118

A man and woman got up in the morning, and whatever he said, he shouldn't have! He got the nose bitten off himself. It was one of those days! So he grabbed his lunchbox and got out of there.

The kids, of course, are not shrewd enough yet. They're walking into straight lefts all over the kitchen. One fella's doing his homework in the middle of the cornflakes, the other fella can't find his socks and somebody else is looking for money for something, which can be very dangerous. Anyhow they eventually get turfed out the door and they're in bad form. They won't even talk to their friends and their friends are annoyed with them. And by lunchtime, what started in the kitchen that morning has gone all over the parish!

Meanwhile, back in the kitchen at eleven o'clock, God love her, she's still in the dressing gown. Ten cigarettes and twelve cups of tea later, it finally dawned on her that nothing that happened in this house this morning could possibly come from God. And that shocked her, because she was a good woman. So she took the bottle of holy water, sprinkled it around the kitchen and told Satan to go to hell. And the cloud lifted, as it always will, and then she phoned her husband and told him it was OK to come home.

I've seen people, I'm sure you have, who have gone down the tube of depression – valium, librium, alcohol – because they keep forgetting the authority that Jesus gives them.

Little Children

119 A father and mother are out for a Sunday walk with junior. As he toddles along, they look back and he is looking in a shop window and they beckon him. He comes waddling along behind and then they look back and he is sitting on the footpath and he's found the cracks and the dirt and he's scraping them with his fingers, and the mother says, 'Oh dirty, ah, ah!' and rubs it off. Then after a while he toddles on ahead of them and there is an intersection coming up. It could be dangerous so they beckon him to wait for them. And eventually he comes to a stage where he just flops down on the footpath, and that's it – he ain't goin' any further! What do they do? The mother just pops him into the pushcar, and continues the journey. Never once do they consider terminating the relationship.

That's the way it is with God. Sometimes we lag behind in guilt and regret, and trying to relive yesterday, and other times we run ahead anticipating the worries of tomorrow, and sometimes we get so tired that we just sit down and can't go any further!

120 *God's gifts are totally free. Will we ever learn that?* Father, mother, junior in a supermarket on a Saturday morning. They get the things they need for the weekend and for the week, and as usual there is always one or two other things that they didn't necessarily come to buy. But as they come to the checkout and begin to put the goods on the conveyor belt, the girl says, 'They're free.' 'What?' 'They're free.' And of course there has to be a catch! The father smiles as he continues to put the items on the conveyor belt. And the girl says again, 'There's no charge.' He thinks, 'Candid Camera!' or there's some catch, some snag. Maybe this girl had a row with the boss, maybe she doesn't work here. He was looking to see could he identify her name-tag. Maybe that guy over there is a store detective. By now he's getting annoyed. It's not funny anymore and he's in a hurry and he's pounding the stuff down on the conveyor belt and he's looking at his wife in amazement and they look – 'Where's junior?' Junior heard the magic words, 'They're free' and he's got another trolley and he's going like a bat out of hell around the supermarket filling that trolley with everything he wants.

Jesus says, you know, 'unless you become like little children, you won't understand what I'm talking about'.

---

121 In the film, *Whistle down the Wind*, a group of children find a tramp in a barn, whom they believe to be Jesus. When their kitten gets sick, they bring him to Jesus and when the kitten dies, they have many questions to ask. 'Why did Jesus let the kitten die?' 'Why do people die?' 'What is this whole business of death?' They run to the nearest church in search of answers. They are ushered into the priest who is having his tea. Their opening question is direct, 'Why does Jesus let people die?' The priest responds with an answer, which is pious, proper and correct. He uses theological words, precise words, God words, as he formulates an orthodox answer. Then he pours himself another cup of tea and seems quite satisfied. As the children walk away, one little boy turns to his older sister and says, 'He doesn't know either, sure he doesn't?'

---

122 'Where did I come from?' the young son asked his father, while in the course of writing an essay. 'Santa Claus brought you,' says the father, who did not believe that all questions really have to be answered. 'And where did you come from?' 'Oh, the stork brought me,' was his father's answer. 'And Grandad, where did he come from?' The father held his ground firmly and replied, 'He was found under a head of cabbage.' The young lad returned to his writing and after a while he closed the copy and went up stairs to bed. The father was puzzled by the suddenness and persistence of the questions, so he checked the boy's copy, where he read, 'After persistent questioning, it is my firm conclusion that there has not been a normal birth in this family for three generations'.

123

Scott Peck calls 'People of the Lie', people who spend their lives blaming other people for their own problems. Paul says, in Galations 5, that we have to learn to live and walk in the Spirit.

In a cartoon, a mother and father were arguing about junior's budding musical career. 'Alright', the father exclaims, 'so he'll grow up to be a Tubo virtuoso! But can't he just take lessons? Does he have to practise?'

124

Someone said, 'Life is a mystery to be lived, not a problem to be solved'.

A pastor once printed this motto at the top of his parish bulletin, 'Life is a love, not a competition.' The rectory telephone rang all day long that Sunday. One caller said, 'You were wrong, life is a competition. It's easy for you to create those nice-sounding mottos but I live in the real world and, take it from me, life is a competition.'

Jesus asks us to trust in the abundant joys that belong to those who live without preoccupation or anxiety over attaining status and prestige.

125

A young army officer in World War 1 graduated as a second lieutenant a year ahead of his time, because officers were needed desperately. This young man, who had barely begun to shave and looked even younger than his age, was assigned to command a platoon of seasoned veterans. It was still dark the first morning he fell out with his command. He called the platoon to attention and immediately a voice from the rear ranks rang out with a passage from the Book of Isaiah, 'And a little child shall lead them.' 'The man who said that, take one step forward,' the lieutenant commanded. Whereupon the entire platoon took one step forward. 'As you were,' said the young officer. The men took one step back and things returned to normal. That evening, as was the custom, members of the platoon checked the company bulletin board to learn what they were to do the next day. The following notice appeared, signed by their young commander: 'Members of the Third Platoon Company A will fall out tomorrow morning in full field equipment for a thirty-five mile hike, and little child shall lead them, riding on a darn big horse. Follow me!'

126

'Merry Christmas!' said the small boy, as he tenderly handed over his Christmas present to his mother. Earlier that Christmas Eve, he had shyly presented himself to a Department Store clerk. 'I would like to buy my mother a new slip for Christmas,' he said bravely. 'Very nice,' the clerk replied, 'But first I shall have to know more about your mother. Tell me is she short or tall?' 'She's ... eh ... she's perfect,' the boy stammered. So the clerk wrapped a slip size 34 for him. A few days later, the mother returned the perfect 34 slip, and exchanged it for a size 52.

127

There's a story told of a grandmother, a mother and a little boy, three generations, who went into a restaurant and sat down to order. The waitress took the grandmother's order, the mother's order, and then turned to the little boy and said, 'What would you like?' The mother immediately said, 'Oh, I'll order for him.' The waitress, without being overly rude, ignored the mother and again said to the little boy, 'What would you like?' Glancing over at his mother, to see how she was reacting to this, the little boy said, 'Eh, hamburger.' 'How would you like your hamburger, with mustard and pickles and the works?' asked the waitress. With his mouth dropping open in amazement now, he said, 'The works, the works.' She went over to the window and she howled the grandmother's order and the mother's order. Then in a very loud voice, she said, 'And a hamburger with the works.' The little boy turned to his mother in utter astonishment and said, 'Mammy, she thinks I'm real.'

This is what happens when we listen to another person. They suddenly become real. They realise that someone cares enough to recognise their worth as a human being.

128

Listen to this case history that appears in Paul Tournier's book, *The Strong and the Weak*. It's the story of a family consisting of a father, a mother and several children. The father had a problem with one of his daughters, a little girl who was very shy, unable to express herself outwardly. The father was an outgoing person and most of the other children were too. He was puzzled and confused about this but he tried to understand. On one occasion he gave his shy little daughter a present. It was an elegant little glass elephant on a gold chain to put around her neck. He put it down on the table in front of her and said, 'I've brought you this present.' Well, she was just overwhelmed. As Tournier said, 'It shone more beautifully than any star of Bethlehem, because it symbolised her father's love for her.' She sat there for several moments staring at this thing, unable to speak. Then she got up and went into the other room to tell her mother what happened.

When she came back she was thunderstruck because she saw her beautiful little elephant dangling from her sister's neck. The father said in a kind of off-handed way, 'Well, you didn't want it so I gave it to your sister.'

Once again, he wasn't listening.

129 Some children had been asked to set the table for dinner and they were selfish little brats. And as they set the table they wrote a note for their mother, 'For setting the table: 50p.'

The mother came in and she was deeply hurt. So she got a huge big sheet of paper and wrote down, 'For carrying you for nine months within my womb, for giving birth to you, for staying up at night when you were sick, for nursing you, for feeding you, for bathing you, for dressing you, for caring for you all over the years, total bill: Nothing. I did that because I loved you.'

130 Two little lads were arguing about prayer – whether God answers prayers or not. One lad jeered, 'Remember last year when you prayed and asked God that you might get a bicycle? Did he answer you then?' The other lad replied, 'Oh yes! He did answer. He said, 'No!'"

'No' is also an answer, and if God was cruel and sadistic, he would answer our every prayer and then have a good laugh at us. I'm sure we often ask for things that are not really for our good. God will always give you what you ask for, unless he has something better to give.

Holiness

131 There was a young lad one time on his way to school and he looked in a sculptor's yard and he saw this huge big hunk of marble there. The sculptor was about to start working. The young lad couldn't wait because he had to keep going. And each day as he passed by, he heard the work going on. The doors were closed. But months later he was passing by and the front door of the sculptor's yard was opened and he looked in. There on the plinth, where the hunk of marble had been, was a tiger, perfect, life-like, muscles, sinew, claws, paws, tail, head – powerful! And he pulled the sculptor by the sleeve and said, 'How did you know there was a tiger in there?'

Now that's what God sees when he looks at us. He knows that we are made in his image and likeness and he surrounds us by all the people who will make us holy. And you say, 'That one?' Yes, she'll make you very patient. 'That one?' Oh yes, he'll make you a good listener yet.

132 *A saint is not someone who's so heavenly as to be no earthly good. Did you ever hear the phrase about a person, 'God, that one's awful scattered', or 'She badly needs to get herself together'? Well, the opposite to that is togetherness or wholeness, or a nicer word for that is holiness.*

There was a young lad one time who decided he'd become a saint. So he went down to the library and looked up all the books he could on saints, and read about as many as he could find. He came across one that did impress him alright. It was Simon Stilotes. He lived on a big pillar down in the town square, so the young lad said, 'Now that's a good sort of a saint to be because if you are going to be a saint you might as well get maximum press coverage for it.' But he didn't have any pillar to climb up on, so he got a chair in the kitchen and he stood on it. His mother came in the back door and nearly knocked him down and he had to move over. His sister tried to get to the fridge and he had to get out of the way and then, after a while, somebody wanted to get to the sink and he was in the way and he had to move over to another place, and somebody came in another place and knocked him down. After a while, he just threw the chair to one side and he walked out the door muttering to himself, 'Ah no, it's just not possible to become a saint at home'.

133 There was a little kid one time in a church with his mammy and she was lighting candles and doing the stations. And he was doing what little toddlers do in church: he was running around the place and examining everything and, after a while, she called him and he didn't answer. She looked up and he was up in the sanctuary looking up at these stained-glass windows. The sun was just streaming through and he was fascinated as he moved his hands back and forth with all the different colours that were on his face, on his hands, on his clothes. The mother said, 'Come on'. Now there was a statue to the right and he said, 'Who is that?' And she said, 'That's holy God.' Another statue, 'Who is that?' 'That's God's holy mother'. So he pointed up at the stained-glass windows, 'Who are they?' And she said, 'They are the saints'. So the next day in play-school the teacher made some reference to saints and your man got all excited. She didn't know what was wrong! He said, 'They're the ones that let the light shine through.'

134 In *The Power and the Glory*, Graham Greene tells of a priest who was condemned to death during an era of religious persecution in Mexico. The terrifying tensions of the priest in latter years had driven him to drink. It was the morning of his death. He crouched on the floor with an empty brandy flask in his hand, trying to remember an Act of Contrition. He was confused. It was not the good death for which he had always prayed. What a fool he had been to think that he was strong enough to stay when others had fled. 'What an impossible fellow I am!' he thought, 'I've done nothing for anybody. I might just as well never have lived.' Tears poured down his face. He was not, at that moment, afraid of damnation. He felt only an immense disappointment because he had to go to God empty handed. It seemed to him, at that moment, that it would have been quite easy to have been a saint. All it would take was a little self-restraint and a little courage. He felt like someone who had missed happiness by seconds at an appointed place. He knew now that, at the end, there was only one thing that counted – to be a saint.

135

Once, long ago, a teacher walked with his student in the courtyard. The teacher who had lost his sight early in life was known as the blind master. As they passed near a large peach tree, the teacher tilted his head in order to miss some low-hanging limbs. The student looked up startled and said, 'Blind master, how is it that you saw those limbs?' The blind master answered, 'To see with the eye is only one sensation. I heard the wind singing softly in the tree's branches. Close your eyes and tell me what you hear. Do you hear your heart beat? Do you hear the foot-fall of the monk across the courtyard? Do you hear the grasshopper at your feet?' The young pupil looked down in astonishment and saw his first grasshopper of the new spring. 'Teacher, how do you hear these things?' the pupil exclaimed. 'Student, how do you not hear them?' the teacher answered.

When it comes to God, the ears that we hear with are the ears of the heart. And indeed when it comes to praying, the organ God gives me to pray with is my heart.

136

In Tolstoy's beautiful story, *Where Love is, God Is,* there is the story of an old cobbler who hears a voice in his sleep one night. The voice tells him that on the very next day the Lord Jesus will visit him. Next morning, he begins his work in a spirit of high expectation as he eagerly awaits the coming of the Lord. But the only visitors he has that day are people in distress. First, there is an emaciated old beggar with a rattling tubercular cough. The old cobbler takes him in, warms him by the fire and gives him food. Next comes a half frozen, thinly clad woman carrying her hungry baby in her arms. She needs food and clothing and the old cobbler obliges. Then an old apple-woman comes. She is terribly upset because a boy has tried to steal her apples. The cobbler knows the boy and he is able to bring the two together and reconcile them. This day has not turned out as expected, but the cobbler has not forgotten the promise of the Lord's visit. Tired now, he falls asleep in his chair and he hears the same voice from the previous night, 'I was hungry and you fed me, I was thirsty and you gave me drink, I was sick and you ministered to me'.

137

Once a village blacksmith had a vision. The angel of the Lord came to him and said, 'The Lord has sent me. The time has come for you to take up your abode in his kingdom.' 'I thank God for thinking of me,' said the blacksmith, 'but as you know, the season for sowing the crops will soon be here. The people of the village will need their ploughs repaired and their horses shod. I don't want to seem ungrateful, but do you think I might put off taking up my abode in the kingdom until I've finished?' The angel looked at him in the wise and loving way of angels, 'I'll see what can be done,' he said, and he vanished. The blacksmith continued with his work and was almost finished when he heard of a neighbour who fell ill right in the middle of the planting season. The next time he saw the angel, the blacksmith pointed towards the barren fields and pleaded with the angel, 'Do you think eternity can hold off a little longer? If I don't finish the job, my friend's family will suffer.' Again the angel smiled and vanished. The blacksmith's friend recovered, but another's barn burned down and a third was deep in sorrow at the death of his wife and the fourth ... and so on. Whenever the angel reappeared, the blacksmith just spread his hands in a gesture of resignation and compassion and drew the angel's eyes to where the sufferings were.

One evening the blacksmith began to think about the angel and how he'd put him off for such a long time. Suddenly he felt very old and tired and said, 'Lord, if you would like to send your angel again, I think I would like to see him now.' He'd no sooner spoken than the angel stood before him. 'If you still want to take me,' said the blacksmith, 'I am now ready to take up my place in the kingdom of the Lord.' And the angel looked at the blacksmith in surprise and smiled, and he said, 'Where do you think you have been all these years?'

138

A wedding is for a day; a marriage is for a lifetime. The young couple set out on a journey, from falling in love to growing into love.

I remember being at the funeral of the father of a priest friend of mine. I had known his father very well, and I always considered both parents my ideal Darby and Joan. The homily from the son consisted of one sentence, but I've never forgotten it, especially as I knew just how true it was. 'My father was married to my mother for fifty-six years,' he said, 'and in that time he really did come to love her.'

What a journey and what a glorious ending!

Death

139 There was a little girl walking through a cemetery with her Dad and she was looking around. They were taking a short-cut through the cemetery and eventually she pointed to the tombstones and graves and said, 'Daddy, what are those?' And he said, 'Well, these were people who lived in those houses down there, one time, and then Holy God sent for them to come off and live in his house with all his angels.' And, as you parents know, when you answer one question you're going to be asked another one. So the eyes looked puzzled for a moment and she said, 'Daddy, did they go off to live in Holy God's house with all his angels?' 'Yes,' he said. I could almost imagine him with fingers crossed, hoping that he'd get away with it. And then suddenly the eyes lit up and she beamed from ear to ear, because children have a remarkable gift of seeing the obvious at times. 'I bet when they went off to live in Holy God's house, this is where they left their clothes.'

She's right. On the morning of the Resurrection, the angel said to the women, 'If you are looking for Jesus he is not here, but come in and I will show you where he left his clothes.'

140 There was a old tramp one time who heard that the King of Kings was coming to the village and he went to meet him. As he waited his turn, his mind was racing like a computer about all the things he was going to ask for. Eventually it was his turn and he was brought into the presence of this great King of Kings, and, before he got saying anything, the King of Kings said, 'Well, what do you have for me?' And he said, 'I don't have anything.' 'But you must have. Everybody has something to give.' The old tramp, at this stage, was really annoyed and furious and he took out an old cloth he had in his pocket, where he had some grains of wheat that he was chewing coming down the road. He took one of the grains of wheat and gave it to the King of Kings. He almost intended to be offensive by the action. And the King of Kings said, 'Thank you very much,' and he turned and walked away and left him there.

Oh well, the tramp went storming out the door behind him and off down the road muttering to himself. About a mile or so down the road, he took out the cloth to get a few grains of wheat to chew. And there in the middle of the grains of wheat was a tiny grain of gold! He struck himself on the forehead and said, 'You fool, why didn't you give it all away?'

It is said that people, at the end of their lives, often realise that they kept far, far, too much for themselves. Because that's what life is: life is about giving away.

---

141 A cow was having a chat with a pig which was very depressed and the cow was concerned in a sort of a matronly way, and wanted to know what's wrong? The pig said that he was a failure. 'What do you mean?' 'Ah, nobody likes me. They haven't a good word to say about me. Even when they insult each other they can't do that without bringing me into it. I heard a mother the other day saying that her son's bedroom was like a pigsty, and somebody was eating like a pig. They can't insult each other without bringing me into it. Now, when they speak about you they wouldn't use words like that.' And the cow said, 'Yeh, but don't you realise the reason for that?' 'No,' said the pig. 'Well' the cow said, 'I give them milk and cheese and butter and ...' And the pig said, 'What about me? I give them bacon and rashers and ham and pork and sausages and ...' The cow said, 'Yes, but there's a big difference in the giving. I give it to them while I'm still alive. In your case they have to kill you to get anything out of you.'

142

There was a very rich man one time who knew a priest who was supposed to have a hot line to God. Very 'holy'. So he decided he go along to this man, very discreetly, and say, 'Father, if you find out something for me, I will contribute to the completion of the renovation of your church.' Now, of course, holy priest and all that he was, he was practical and the idea of getting the debt cleared was very tempting. So he wanted to know, 'What is it that you want me to do?' 'Well,' he said, 'if you can find out for me will I go to heaven when I die.' So the priest said, 'O.K. It seems strange but I will.' Some days later he came back and he said to the priest, 'Have you any news for me?' And the priest said, 'I have, yes. I have good news and bad news. Which do you want to hear first?' 'Give me the good news, what's the good news?' 'The good news is that, yes, you are going to heaven when you die.' 'Yipee! That's great! But you did say there's bad news – what's the bad news?' 'The bad news is you're going tonight.'

Everybody wants to go to heaven but nobody wants to die

143

There were these grubs at the bottom of a pond and they were discussing among themselves what it was like up there on top of the lily-pond, where many of their brothers are called from time to time. The next one who is called agrees to come back and tell the others what it's like. So this little grub finds himself drawn by nature up to the surface, and when he gets up on the surface of the lily pond, 'It is real bright up here! It's real warm up here!' Then suddenly, he opens out and opens out, and becomes a beautiful dragonfly, which, of course, he was intended to be. He's flying back and forth across the pond and he can see them below. They can't seem him and there is no way he can get back to them. After a while he gives up trying and says, 'Sure, even if they could see me they would never, ever recognise a beautiful creature like me as being one of them.'

'Eyes have not seen nor ear heard nor has it entered into the heart of man to imagine what God has in store for those who love him.'

144

This man died and was brought to a place which was really quite good. He was hungry and a little guy came in and gave him something to eat. He was thirsty, a little guy came in and gave him something to drink. He was tired, a little guy came in, pressed a button and a bed came out of the wall. He lay down and went to sleep. Anything he thought he wanted, he got it; he half wanted it, he was given it; he wished for it and it was offered to him. This went on and eventually he stopped this young lad and he said, 'Excuse me! Can you do without anything here?' and the lad said, 'Oh, no, no, no!' 'Even things you only half want or don't really want?' 'Oh, no, no, no!' he said, 'you have to have them.' And the man said, 'I mean, is this going to go on for all eternity?' 'Oh, yes. Yes, it is.' And he said, 'Ah, Lord, I'd be better off in hell!' And the little guy said, 'And where do you think you are?'

Quite often hell, for some people on this earth, is that they have too much and therefore they lose what is most precious in life – a sense of appreciation and a sense of gratitude for what they have.

145

'There are three things that will surprise you when you get to heaven. You'll be surprised at some of the people you'll see there. You'll be surprised at some of the people who won't be there. And the biggest surprise of all will be to find yourself there.'

I would hasten to add, of course, that if you are surprised at some of the people you see there, that's a judgment and I'd advise you to look around! Maybe you're not in heaven at all!

146

I remember one lovely, simple soul who was dying of cancer. I was with her on the Friday and I was convinced that she was not going to be here when I came back on Monday. So I prayed with her and gave her absolution. I even joked and said I gave her absolution for all the things she hadn't time to do! I blessed her with oil and said, 'Now, Annie, pet, your bags are packed and if the Lord comes looking for you at the weekend, away with you! You're all set.' And then I said to her, very seriously, 'Sure you won't be afraid to meet him?' and her answer was instant and from her heart: 'Father, I'm sure he's going to be awful glad to see me.'

The saint is not the person who loves God. The saint is the person who is totally convinced that God loves her.

147

I remember seeing a poster one time which said, 'Please send me the flowers when I can still smell them.'

There is always a tendency to keep them and put them on the coffin. And they're really no good to anyone then.

148

On a tomb-stone was written the words:
'Remember stranger as you pass by
as you are now so once was I.
As I am now so you shall be
so prepare yourself to follow me.'
Some wit wrote with a chalk down at the bottom:
'To follow you I'm quite content
but how do I know which way you went?'

149

There was a king, who was a proper king, and he had a fool, who was a proper fool. One day the king gave a staff to the fool and told him to hold on to it until he met a bigger fool than himself. Years passed. The king was dying. He sent for all his courtiers, servants, attendants, including the fool, to take his leave. He said he was going on a long journey and would not be coming back. The fool asked, 'Majesty, before this, whenever you went on a journey to a foreign kingdom, you always sent soldiers and servants ahead of you to prepare the way, and to have everything in proper order. May I ask what preparations you have made for this journey which you are going to undertake?' 'Alas,' said the king, 'I have been too long doing other things, and I have made no preparations.' 'Well,' said the fool, 'take this staff, for at last I have met a bigger fool than myself!'

150

Jesus came to let us join our living and our dying to his.
There is an Indian legend about a tribe from the great lakes. They had a long-standing tradition of sacrificing one of their maidens each year to the great god of the waters, whom they deeply feared. The practice was to draw lots among the most beautiful maidens and the one selected was put into the river above Niagara Falls and ordered to go over the Falls as a human sacrifice. The chief of the tribe was a good man who loved his family, and you can imagine his feelings one year when his own daughter drew the lot. He could not violate the custom of his tribe. When the fateful day came, the chief could not be found to preside over the ceremony. Some of the tribesmen began to murmur against him, saying that he could no longer be trusted to fulfil his responsibilities as chief. Finally, as the day's end drew near, they realised they would have to go ahead with the ceremony without the chief or the tradition would be broken. So they put the chief's beautiful daughter into the canoe and pushed it out into the river. As they did so, they saw another canoe coming onto the river out of the bushes where it had been concealed. In the gathering twilight they recognised the person in the other canoe as their chief, the girl's father. Suddenly both canoes were caught in a swift current at the centre of the river and they went over the Falls together.